Count My
Many Blessings

Count My Many Blessings

(They're in There Somewhere)

John Stanfield

VANTAGE PRESS
New York

FIRST EDITION

All rights reserved, including the right of
reproduction in whole or in part in any form.

Copyright © 2002 by John Stanfield

Published by Vantage Press, Inc.
516 West 34th Street, New York, New York 10001

Manufactured in the United States of America
ISBN: 0-533-14162-1

Library of Congress Catalog Card No.: 01-130492

0 9 8 7 6 5 4 3 2 1

In honor of my mother and daddy, my brothers Freeman and W.T., my sister Rebecca, and my cousin Floyd Outlaw.

Dedicated to my sisters Margaret, Bettie, Bee, and Pat.

With special thanks to my wife, Tolva, whose interest and insistence compelled me to write down these memories of my early years.

Contents

1. Genesis — 1
2. Harris Hooper's Place — 10
3. Birmingham — 20
4. Back to the Old Home Place — 35
5. The Creek — 47
6. Hard Scrabble — 54
7. School — 61
8. Danger — 71
9. Interlude — 77
10. W.T.'s Christmas — 81
11. Exodus — 88
12. The Magic City — 92
13. Floyd, Oretta, and the 5-Minute War — 97
14. West End — 100
15. Revolting Hormones — 106
16. East Point — 110
17. School, Magic, Bike, and Boat — 115
18. Selling Wood, Football, Boxing, and Girls — 120
19. Vacations and Girls — 124
20. The Texas Connection — 128
21. Increasing Income — 131
22. Freeman, Me, and W.T. — 135
23. Last Year at Russell — 139
24. Post Graduation — 143
25. Fort Sill — 149
26. A.S.T.P. — 152
27. Camp Maxey — 159
28. Shipping Out — 166
29. This Is It — 173

30.	Battle of the Bulge	179
31.	Scenes of War	187
32.	Baths and R & R	191
33.	I Make Corporal; Germans Surrender!	195
34.	Back in the States	201
35.	Macon, after the War	205
36.	The East Point Commune	211

Epilogue   235

Count My
Many Blessings

1
Genesis

In 1910 the Fry family moved from White Oak to Trinity, a farm community about seven miles northwest of Waverly, Tennessee, along Clydeton Road. Having learned that there were six daughters in the family, many of the young men of the area managed to be near the house they were moving into when their wagon arrived. When the girls got down off the wagon, Charlie Stanfield, who was among the spectators, commented to his companions, "I'm gonna marry that tall one."

The tall one was Luttie Victoria. About four years later, Charlie made good on his promise, marrying the tall woman who was to become my mother. At the time he married, Daddy was the last of eight children still living with his parents on the farm where he was born, a quarter-mile off Clydeton Road on the remote side of Big Richland Creek. When they married, he and mother moved to Jackson, Tennessee, where Daddy had gone to work with the Mobile & Ohio Railway. They lived temporarily with one of Daddy's brothers, who also worked for the railroad, but before they found a residence of their own Daddy was "laid off." This was not a total misfortune because his father needed him to help harvest the crop that year, so he and Mother moved back into the old home place.

February 1, 1915, Dr. W.R. Horner, who lived six

miles west on Clydeton Road, drove his horse and buggy across Big Richland Creek to deliver their first child, Charles Freeman.

When Freeman was about six months old, Daddy and Mother took him by horse and buggy to Danville, about a day's journey, to visit Mother's sister, Aunt Kate Outlaw. While they were gone the rains came and every valley in Humphreys county spilled into Big Richland Creek, which flooded its banks and rushed tumultuously toward the Tennessee River. By the time they returned the waters had receded to some extent, but the creek was still swollen and flowing swiftly. The creek flowed generally east to west. Daddy drove up Highway 5 (Clydeton Road) to the point where the highway bridge crossed the creek and let Mother and Freeman out on the south side. This point was around two miles from the old home place, and there was no road and not even a continuous path through the fields and hills between. But Mother was used to walking, and resolutely began the trek along the creek bank.

Daddy drove back down the gravel highway and across the lane to the creek. The ford was now wide and threatening, but by angling upstream, he judged that he would be able to cross. He clicked his tongue and snapped the reins against the horse's rump. Obediently, the horse waded in, but at midstream he suddenly found his feet would not reach bottom. With eyes flaring in terror, he paddled furiously. A while later his hooves touched bottom again and he emerged dripping and snorting, drawing the buggy behind. Unnoticed by Daddy until Mother arrived, the travel trunk that had been on the back of the buggy had been washed away when the waters rose above the buggy bed and, by then, was probably in the Tennessee River. That trunk contained their extra clothes, including Mother's best dress and a brand new hat given to her by Aunt Kate. Even more heartbreaking, it also contained a "precious" letter she had taken to Danville to show to Aunt Kate. It had been written by Aunt Betty to baby Freeman. Mother cried.

Even though Daddy's parents were "good to her," Mother was not completely happy. She and Daddy had discussed the possibility of moving, but Daddy felt obligated to help his father with the farm. There was nowhere they could move and still be close enough for him to do so. One day when Mother went to check for mail she "sat a while" with Mr. Bryant and Miss Annie on the front porch of their log house, which was adjacent to the RFD* mailbox on Clydeton Road. She was delighted to learn from them that Mrs. Kinney, recently widowed, was moving and that her little house, only a half mile from the old home place, would become available. In her own words**, she "jumped like lightning" to get back across the creek to tell Daddy. She walked down to the field where he was digging peanuts and said, "Charlie, we're gonna move!"

They had to acquire everything needed to "set up housekeeping." Mrs. Kinney sold them a wood-burning cook stove (which also furnished heat), a table and two chairs. Grandmother furnished them a bedstead. Daddy went to the general store to buy ticking for a shuck mattress. When he returned with the ticking, he was carrying a bucket and dipper. When Mother asked what in the world he was doing with a bucket and dipper, he said, "That's the only thing I could think of that we can't do without."

*Rural Free Delivery.
**From an audio tape recorded about 1980.

Their new home was a two-room cabin, complete with open-air toilet facilities and running water only a hundred yards away. Daddy, having grown up in a four-room house with very similar facilities, was quite comfortable. After all, as he said many times, "All anybody needs is a room and a side room." But Mother's father had been a merchant who owned a general store and a "landing" on the Tennessee River. So she had grown up with considerably more luxuries. Of course luxuries from 1890 to 1914 were a far cry from what they are today. In any case, she was a strong woman, measuring only a couple of inches less than Daddy's six-feet-one, with an inherited German determination, and she set about at once to make the two rooms into a home.

Sometime before December 1916, however, the Sykes' house became available. This was a neat five-room house, painted white, on Clydeton Road, separated only by a pasture from the lane leading to Daddy's old home. With another baby due, Mother needed the warmth and comfort of a better house, so they jumped at this opportunity. Their second child, William Thomas (W.T.) was born in the Sykes' house Christmas Day, 1916.

In 1917, because of age and poor health, Daddy's parents moved to Nashville to live with their youngest daughter, Aunt Betty. Mother and Daddy moved back to the old home place. We know this was sometime before W.T. was a year or so old, for there is a photo showing him and Freeman in the front yard being shepherded by two Collie dogs. Mother delighted in bragging about the intelligence of those dogs and the way they would accompany the children and prevent them from wandering off toward the creek.

Dr. Horner, driving a horse and buggy, and then a Model-T Ford, forded Big Richard Creek five times in the next few years to deliver two more boys and three girls. One of the boys, Rex Dudley, died as an infant, but Sarah Rebecca, Margaret Nell, John Calvin, and Betty Lois survived. "Survived," for the whole family, is a most appropriate word considering that there were eight people in a four-room house with no plumbing, no electricity, and no heat except for a wood-burning cook stove and a fireplace. The roof was wood shingles, the floors were a single thickness, and the walls consisted of wide boards nailed horizontal on the inside and vertical on the outside with narrow strips over the cracks. There was no insulation between. And there in middle Tennessee the winters could be quite cold.

There was one neighbor, the Forrests, about a half-mile up the creek, but there was no connecting roadway—only a path along the creek, through one wide field and two orchards and over one very steep hill. In the other direction, down the creek, there were no houses all the way to the Tennessee River, some five miles away. The only access to the outside world was a foot log over the creek when it was at normal level, and a rudimentary swinging bridge about halfway to the Forrest's place, which could be used when the foot log was washed out.

It was a hard life. By working daylight to dark, Daddy managed to raise enough to feed the family, but not to accumulate anything at all. With seven children to care for, cooking, washing, milking the cow and helping care for the garden, Mother probably worked even harder than Dad. Yet Daddy managed to buy her a Singer sewing machine and she managed to become an expert seamstress, not only making clothes for the children, but for the neighbors as well.

Not only was life hard, but it was probably boring as well. Maybe not for Dad, because he was so tired after a day plowing, clearing land or chopping stove wood that he was ready to sit, read an outdated newspaper and go to bed. Also, he had spent almost his entire life in this house, and a fractional but strong strain of Indian blood perhaps contributed to his contentment with the backwoods isolation and the unhurried atmosphere in which they lived. But Mother missed the coming and going of people in the general store her father ran, and the excitement of showboats on the river. She missed people. Someway, two or three times a week, she would find time in the middle of all her chores to walk the foot log and the quarter-mile lane to check the RFD mailbox and perhaps spend a few minutes with the Bryants.

Daddy's father, Newton Calvin Stanfield, died April 17, 1919. Daddy went to Nashville for the funeral. When he returned he found the creek had flooded to the point that it almost reached the house. All his "bottom land" planted with corn and peanuts was underwater. By the time the creek receded and the land dried out it would be too late for him to plant again. This loss of his crops and many weeks of hard labor, added to his grief over his father's death, utterly overwhelmed him. When she told about this incident, Mother said it was the only time she ever saw Daddy cry.

Mother constantly felt the loneliness of the rustic board-and-batten household tucked back in the wild, separated from the world by a sometimes impassable creek. And at time she felt fear. She told of a frightening experience one night when Daddy was away, possibly at the time he was in Nashville for his father's funeral. The lamp had been blown out and the children were asleep when she heard an eerie caterwauling sound, which seemed to be circling the house. As she listened it seemed to be getting closer and closer. She remembered tales of rabid catamounts or wildcats making ferocious attacks and her hair stood on end. Her common sense told her a catamount would not attempt to break into a house, but the inhuman screaming argued otherwise and she was suddenly very conscious of the unlocked doors. She found Daddy's shot gun and, trembling with fear, stood waiting for the sound of something attempting to push its way in. Then the eerie sounds began to recede. But still she spent a sleepless night.

Undoubtedly, it was loneliness and fear, as well as a desire for a good school for the children and a better life for all that resulted in a move from the old home place to a house in town.

Waverly was not a large town; not too much more than "a wide place in the road" on U.S. Highway 78 about halfway between Nashville and Memphis. Highway 78, Main Street, was narrow enough that the maple trees on each side almost met, forming a picturesque archway through the center of town. There was a courthouse square and perhaps fifteen or twenty places of business, but two blocks away from the square, the houses were on large lots with gardens and not a few chickens, horses and cows. Aunt Betty Forrest's place included a full-size barn. So Daddy and Mother with their six children, chickens, a cow and a horse were not out of place.

There was little opportunity for employment. Daddy eked out a living doing odd jobs, mainly plowing gardens for those who did not have a horse and plow. On two occasions Daddy left the family to work in other cities. I do not know exactly when, but it's logical to assume that it was during the brief time that they were living in Waverly. Once he took a job in Nashville as a streetcar conductor. Immediately after one of his first paydays he was walking down the street in broad daylight when someone stuck a gun in his back and robbed him of every cent he had. Distraught and discouraged, he quit his job and took a Greyhound bus back to Waverly.

On another occasion, he went to Akron, Ohio, and took a job in a factory making hot water bottles. For someone accustomed to working outside at farmer speed, the hustle of the assembly line was unbearable, and he burned his hands on the hot rubber to such an extent that he carried scars to his dying days. So it was not long before he was on the bus back south. I never heard Daddy or Mother mention this episode, but W.T. told me about it seventy-two years later, in 1999.

It was difficult for someone who, as Daddy himself used to say "had a second-grade education" to find work aside from his lifelong occupation of farming. Whether he actually attended school only two years I'm not sure, but even though his formal education was extremely limited, he was a very intelligent man and he obtained a good practical education by reading every newspaper he could get his hands on. Apparently, while he was growing up, reading and studying was the norm at home. He used to talk a lot about studying the Bible and early historians, such as Flavius Josephus. For a while, the old home place was the meeting place for a congregation of the Church of Christ, then known as the Christian Church. But from the time Daddy married, the lack of local preachers, and the ordeal of providing for his growing family, hindered any formal religious activity for many years.

After a year or so in town it became obvious to Daddy that available employment could not sustain his family of eight. I suspect there was difficulty in paying the rent. So the decision was made to move back to the old home place. Their furniture was loaded in a wagon and they were on their way when someone informed Daddy that Harris

Hooper was looking for someone to live on his farm as a sharecropper. Daddy was familiar with the Hooper place, a large farm on the Tennessee River with rich bottom land, and a fine house and barn. Arrangements were hastily made and, instead of turning at the lane, the wagon took their furniture on down Clydeton Road about five miles to the Harris Hooper Place.

That was in 1927. I was four years old, and my memories begin at this point.

2
Harris Hooper's Place

The house was white, two stories, with a long hall separating the right from the left. There was a spacious porch at the front and back; a large level yard at the front, and a smaller level yard then a steep hill in the back. To the left of the house, was a hillside pasture with a stock pond about halfway up. To the right, a dry creek bed led back between two hills into the woods. One of my first memories is playing in that creek bed with my cousin, Richard Jernigan. We were just beginning to discover the wonders of the world and we found one of them in that creek bed—a rock wonderfully shaped like a bird.*

The house faced the gravel roadway, called Highway 5 or Clydeton Road, and across the road was a wide wood gate leading into the barnyard and, behind a huge sweet gum tree, a large red barn. A pasture with grazing horses and cattle was to the right of the barn, and beyond that were the fields of bottom land, then trees marking the banks of the Tennessee River.

It seems that it was not long after we moved into the Harris Hooper Place that I got a new baby sister. No one

---

*In 1999 I saw Richard for the first time in 72 years. One of his first questions was, "Do you remember the rocks we found in the dry branch at Harris Hooper's place?"

told me where she came from, but I remember that Aunt Kate was there, so maybe she brought her. I remember first seeing her in a baby bed in the back bedroom, which was on the right side of the house with windows looking out onto the back porch. Mother, Aunt Kate and a number of other female people (probably Aunt Betty and perhaps my older sisters, Margaret and Rebecca) were also there. A discussion was going on as to what the baby should be named. There was general agreement that she should be named after Aunt Bert, mother's sister, Bertha. But there was disagreement and prolonged discussion as to what her second name should be. Someone suggested "Louise" but others objected, saying they did not like the sound of "Bertha Louise." Becoming fed up with the back-and-forth comments, I spoke up and said, "Why not call her Bertha Lou?"

Everybody laughed—in those days children were supposed to be seen and not heard—but then everyone agreed to that name. Except Bertha Lou. She could not speak at the time, but she let me know in later years that she did not appreciate the name at all and, in fact, when she was about sixteen, issued an edict that she would henceforth be known as "Bee."

Thinking of that bedroom and the windows opening onto the back porch reminds me of another incident which occurred about that same time. I was on the back porch, apparently feeling quite jolly, and began dancing and singing "Hand Me Down My Walking Cane," which I found to be a very amusing song. Suddenly I heard laughter and felt my face burning with embarrassment as I realized the adults were looking at me through the bedroom windows. The fact that I never became a famous song-and-dance man can be traced directly back to that incident.

But I did continue at intervals to sing "Hand Me Down My Walking Cane." Another of my four-year-old memories is standing in the front yard at Harris Hooper's Place and teaching that song to my cousin Richard, who was about my age. Nobody in my family drank alcohol. However, I remember hearing jokes about Daddy doing so before he was married. And perhaps it was from those jokes that I learned what was meant by a "bottle of corn." My favorite line in this song was "Hand me down my bottle of corn; I'm gonna get drunk as sure as you're born." To me, at four years of age, that was hilarious.

There being no television, radio or record players, songs were learned by word of mouth, simply passed along by friends or learned at "musicals," parties where local fiddlers, guitar and banjo players entertained. There were Victrolas, but we were not prosperous enough to own one. And radios were just being introduced in rural areas. The Stanfills, who lived a few miles down Clydeton Road, were the first we knew to get a radio. One night our whole family walked down to their house for the express purpose of seeing this new-fangled machine. It was a big box with knobs on it sitting against a wall. I was absolutely amazed to hear music coming from that box. I finally figured out that there were little people inside, playing little banjos, fiddles and guitars. But apparently the Stanfills didn't want us to know that. They told us the music was coming from something called *The Grand Old Opry* in Nashville, and they had the box against the wall so we couldn't see inside. I was too polite to give them away.

My first memory of my brother Freeman is hearing him talk with Cecil Stanfill about learning to play the guitar. Both of them did learn. In fact Freeman became a guitar teacher and I suspect his inspiration came from that big box with the little people inside.

My first memory of my brother W.T. involves watching him in the hillside pasture at Harris Hooper's Place playing with a pet goat. When T turned his back the goat would butt him vigorously, sometimes lifting him off the ground. T would just laugh, or fuss at the goat playfully. But I watched apprehensively through a fence between the pasture and the yard and resolved never to get on the same side of the fence with that goat. I guess it could have been called cowardice on my part but, now that I know the word, I prefer to call it "prudence."

Even at that early age of four or five I had someway developed a fear of being called a coward or "sissy." Perhaps it was because of some teasing about the fact that I liked to go into Margaret and Rebecca's bedroom, which was an upstairs room on the right side of the house, and watch them play with their paper dolls. They cut the dolls from the Sears and Roebuck catalog, along with dresses, hats and shoes. They would lay the dolls on their bed, and I found it fascinating to see the way they fastened on the dresses, etc., by folding over little tabs they had left when they cut them out. I wish I had thought at the time to explain that this was a scientific interest in seeing the way the clothing was attached. I hereby present this defense.

As a further defense against the possibility of being perceived as a four-year-old sissy, let me mention an incident that I don't actually remember, but heard Mother tell about many times. It seems the first Christmas we were at Harris Hooper's Place Santa Claus, being extremely busy and probably a little hard-pressed for cash, forgot to bring a present for me. Discovering this at the last minute, he put my name on an extra doll that was available, and it was presented to me while I was still in bed Christmas morning. I looked at the doll contemptuously, then proceeded to throw it across the room against the wall. I don't know what Santa brought me the following Christmas, but I'm reasonably sure it was not a doll. I'm absolutely sure that present-day psychologists are ridiculous when they claim that differences in preferences between boys and girls are learned rather than natural.

One day shortly after my fifth birthday, I went to the field with Daddy—probably sent by Mother to reduce the number of children in the house—and sat playing in the shade of a tree while he plowed. Because of recent rains, the Tennessee River was out of its banks and considerably closer to the field than it normally would be. Margaret and Rebecca, along with cousins Ruth and Mary Ellen Jernigan, were playing in Mr. Hooper's fishing boat tied up nearby. Suddenly screams of terror broke the pastoral silence. Daddy dropped his plow handles and started running toward the river and I, not knowing anything else to do, chased after him. As we arrived at the water's edge, Rebecca, wet and distraught, still in water above her waist, was struggling for the bank pulling the boat with one hand behind her. The other girls were sitting in the boat screaming shrilly.

After calming the girls, Daddy discovered they had decided to go for a ride in the boat, but had drifted farther from shore than they intended. In their excitement, they dropped the one paddle overboard. As they continued drifting outward they started screaming. Rebecca, at ten years old captain of the crew, jumped from the boat to pull it to shore. She went in over her head, but had finally found her footing on the muddy bottom by the time Daddy arrived. He helped her pull the boat to the bank and the frightened girls scrambled out. However, the paddle was floating far out in the water, drifting faster downstream as it got into the main current.

Daddy asked me if I wanted to go with him to retrieve the paddle. Surveying the surly, muddy water, my inborn prudence (as we will refer to it henceforth) told me "No," but being one of the two men present, I felt obligated to go and climbed into the boat. Daddy pushed off into the deep water then, getting to the front of the boat and bending over with one arm on each side of the prow, paddled with his hands until he reached the paddle. Then he paddled easily back to shore and I, feeling quite brave and manly, basked in imagined admiration by the girls.

In the melee, Mary Ellen lost a prized piece of jewelry. Perhaps because of this, the story has been retold many times both in the Stanfield and the Jernigan families* Incredibly, however, my intrepid role has been largely ignored.

Generally, we stayed away from the river. So the real danger it presented was not drowning but disease. Because of bites from mosquitoes bred in the backwaters, we were constantly suffering from chills and fever. Among my early recollections are the visits by Aunt Betty Forrest and Aunt Arbie Jernigan when we were sick. The main things I remember are the oranges and bananas they would bring, such rare and delicious treats that they made it almost worth being sick.

On one occasion when I was suffering with chills and fever and I was in bed in the front bedroom and could hear the droning sound of the adults in another part of the house. Then, although I could not even remember get-

---

*In the Jernigan version, Mary Ellen jumped out of the boat. Perhaps both she and Rebecca did.

ting out of bed, the adults found me standing on the back porch. They carried me back to bed, exclaiming in alarm that I must be delirious from my high fever. But they did not summon a doctor. All of us had repetitive bouts with fever, which must have been akin to malaria, but I don't remember ever having a doctor when these fevers occurred. Dr. Horner lived reasonably near on Clydeton Road but, having no telephone, we could summon him only by walking the two or three miles to his home. So usually we relied on home remedies: rest in bed, chest rubs with Vicks salve or turpentine, or a dose of castor oil. If the doctor came, we could expect quinine, Black Draught or Epsom salts.

On one occasion W.T. swallowed a fish bone, which became stuck in his throat. Although he didn't seem to be in great distress, Mother insisted that he go to see Dr. Horner. I walked with him down the gravel road to the doctor's house. After peering down his throat, Dr. Horner prescribed corn bread. We were impressed with the simplicity of the remedy, but we were more impressed by the fact that Dr. Horner made no charge. Perhaps he decided he had made enough delivering babies for mother that it was appropriate to treat a stuck bone *pro bono*.

The most bizarre incident pertaining to health happened to Margaret. She, Rebecca, W.T. and Freeman attended school at the Cragg Schoolhouse, a one-room building a mile or so from Harris Hooper's Place. One day when Margaret was in the second grade, she was "reciting," standing in the front of the room reading, when a most discomforting feeling began to rise in her throat. Suddenly she gagged and ejected an eight-inch-long tapeworm. The teacher placed the worm in a fruit jar, probably for her to take home to show her parents. Margaret is now eighty-one years old, but this embarrassing episode is still vivid in her mind.

I was too young to understand our relationship with Mr. Hooper, and still know only that Daddy took care of his live stock and cultivated his farm in exchange for some portion of the proceeds. Even though we were living in a comfortable house and did not lack for food, apparently Daddy and Mother were not completely happy with the relationship. On Mother's part, it may have been because we had to care for Mr. Hooper's dog, Blue Bones.

Mr. Hooper liked to hunt, but his wife objected to his dogs. When he bought Blue Bones he was afraid to let her know about it, so he asked Daddy to keep the dog for him. Blue Bones was a large, gangly hound with a penchant for knocking things over and causing trouble any way he could. Perhaps the best example was the time when Mother left a baked hen sitting on the kitchen table and, when no one was in the room, Blue Bones broke through the screen door, clambered up onto the table and devoured a good portion of the hen before Mother drove him off with a broom. So it could be that it was not completely unintentional when Mrs. Hooper was visiting one day and Mother "let it slip" that Blue Bones actually belonged to Mr. Hooper. However, Mother is the one who told me this story, and she said that she did not know that Mrs. Hooper thought the dog belonged to Daddy.

There was one other incident, which led me to perceive intuitively, even at my early age, that Mother might not be too friendly with Mr. Hooper. He had dropped by and he and Daddy were standing beside the barnyard gate talking. Mother had supper on the table and was waiting impatiently for Daddy to come in, occasionally peering out the front door with a disapproving look. Finally she sent me out with instructions to tell him supper was ready. This being 1928, most children were hesitant to interrupt their elders and I, because of my aforementioned prudence, particularly so. I approached the two men, who naturally paid no attention to me whatsoever, and stood there in a dilemma, wondering how I was going to obey one parent without offending the other. Daddy and Mr. Hooper continued to talk, with never a pause long enough for me to give my message, which I had rehearsed over and over in my mind. Finally, in desperation, I tugged at Daddy's overalls and said meekly, "Mother said supper is ready."

Mr. Hooper immediately said he had to be going. They ended the conversation, and we went in to supper.

Of more substance, for both Daddy and Mother, was discontent with the fact that they were earning food and shelter, but little else. And the poor prospect that there would ever be more. Our health problems undoubtedly concerned them as well.

Sometime earlier, Aunt Kate and Uncle Will Outlaw, with their family, had moved to Birmingham, Alabama, a city that was growing so phenomenally that it was known as the Magic City. Mother's father, grandfather Fry who was living in Austin, Texas, had visited Aunt Kate in Birmingham, and both of them wrote Daddy urging him to go there to check out the prospect of a job. So Daddy took a train down to Birmingham and went to work for the American Creosote Company. It was a hard-labor job, "peeling" telephone poles by hand with a drawing knife, but it paid more than he had ever imagined he would make. As soon as he saved enough money he sent it to mother and, with the help of Aunt Betty and Uncle Tom Forrest, she had our furniture boxed and shipped by freight train, then boarded a passenger train with her seven children headed for the Magic City.

This was in 1929. The Great Depression was lurking in the shadows and I don't suppose there could have been a worse time to make such a move.

3
Birmingham

A ride on a train was so unique, and was undoubtedly so exciting, that I should remember it in great detail. Strangely, however, I cannot remember the ride or arriving in Birmingham at all. I do remember moving into the marvelous white house on 51st Street. It was the first time I had seen an inside bathroom and electric lights.

I'm sure that Mother was the happiest one of all. She would still cook on a wood-burning stove and wash clothes in an iron pot in the back yard and we still did not have a telephone. But for heat there was a coal-burning grate in every room, and a spigot in the backyard to fill her washtubs and iron pot. She no longer had to go to an outside toilet, no longer had to tote water from a spring, no longer had to bathe in a washtub and no longer had to sew by the light of a kerosene lamp. There was a modern grocery store one block away, streetcars to the city within walking distance and a large modern school almost within sight.

The house was second from the end on 51st Street, which ended at a wooded area that separated the residential area from the American Creosote Company. Daddy could walk to and from work, and even come home for lunch. It was a back-breaking job, bending over telephone poles laid side by side on slightly raised ramps, and using a drawing knife to cut off the bark remaining after the poles went through a peeling machine. Fortunately, he did not come into direct contact with the pungent creosote with which the poles were pressure-treated after being peeled. And very shortly he was promoted from peeling poles to cutting "gains." These were flattened slots into which cross arms were fastened when the poles were installed. Making them involved sawing the slots to the proper depth then cutting with a foot adz, which was like a hoe-shaped ax, and then drilling a bolt hole from the center of the "gain" through the pole. For the cross arms to fit properly, the gains had to be perfectly made. This required a good eye and a deft hand. Daddy gained quite a reputation for his skill in this and other work involved in making poles.

Bettie and Bertha (this was before her mandate changing her name) were still too young for school, but the population at Central Park School increased by five on our arrival. The first school day, Mother pointed us in the direction of the school and we were on our own. Freeman, 16, W.T., 13, Rebecca, 11, Margaret, 8 and me, 6. I'm sure the older ones helped Margaret and me to some extent, but they were not exactly sophisticated, having had only a few years education in a one-room school and no "city" experience whatsoever.

Fortunately for me, my first-grade teacher Miss Burglar was a sensitive, loving lady. I suppose it was the first time I had ever been completely separated from my family, so it was a traumatic experience. The thing I remember most is that we sat in the classroom for what seemed an eternity and I had a most urgent need to go to the outhouse. Having no idea as to the proper procedure in that situation when in custody, I sat there until the natural consequence occurred. Eventually seeing my predicament, Miss Burglar said to another little boy, "Billy, I don't think anyone showed John where the bathroom is. Would you show him?"

Even at the time I recognized, and appreciated, her diplomacy and consideration.

Billy Thomas guided me down a long hallway to the bathroom at the far end of the building and at the same time became the first friend, other than my cousins, that I had ever had.

Billy lived in the same direction as I and we began walking part way home and to school together. On the way, we passed Marino's candy store, and whenever one of us had a penny we would stop in to buy five Silver Bells, two Tootsie Rolls or a Hollaway. A Hollaway was a small caramel, similar to a tootsie roll but rectangular. Some of them had a white core, and when you got one of those you won a large Brown Cow sucker. Billy pointed out to me that the winner Hollaways were somewhat smaller than the others—probably because the white core shrank more than the caramel. We won a remarkable number of Brown Cows, but not too consistently lest Mr. Marino should discover our secret. I now suspect that he knew our secret all along.

Since the grocery store was only a block away, mother sometimes sent me to buy groceries. Two men ran the grocery store and one of them would collect the merchandise one item at a time as you told him what was wanted. Mother would give me a list, which I would give to the man behind the counter. From comments the two men made to each other, I sensed that they thought we were "country hicks." On one occasion I was greatly embarrassed when one of them, ignoring me as if I were too young or too stupid to understand, laughingly read mother's list to the other, "She wants twelve b-a-n-a-s and a bar of 'tub' soap."

For seventy-two years I have at intervals thought of what I should have said in response. "Everybody abbreviates words on a grocery list. My mother graduated from high school and certainly knows how to spell 'bananas.' And, as for 'tub' soap, that's a perfectly reasonable way to differentiate between toilet soap and soap that's used in a washtub. Furthermore, your wife wears army shoes."

At the time, however, I didn't know the words "abbreviate" or "differentiate" and I didn't know that mother had graduated from high school, which was a rare thing in her day. Also, I hadn't yet learned that zinger about army shoes.

Sometimes when I went to the store the groceries on Mother's list would fill two large paper sacks and would be a little too heavy for me to carry. I developed a leap-frog system of setting one bag down on the sidewalk, carrying the other forward a hundred feet or so, setting it down and returning for the other one. However, this difficulty led me to develop a business plan, which I think would have been hugely successful except that I couldn't get financing. My idea was to buy a little red wagon to deliver groceries not only for Mother but for the neighbors as well. I presented the plan to Mother in my most persuasive manner, but she didn't buy it—neither the plan nor the little red wagon. The fact that I am not now the owner of a nationwide fleet of delivery trucks can be traced directly back to this incident.

I've wondered why Mother sent me to the store so often rather than Freeman or W.T. Being considerably older, thirteen and fifteen, they were perhaps involved in more important things. I know that while we were still on 51st Street Freeman someway obtained a used bicycle and got a job delivering for a drugstore. And not too long after that he dropped out of school to work full time to help support the family. This was in 1929–30, the beginning of the Great Depression and the creosote plant had cut back the hours that Daddy worked more and more as "hard times" arrived.

I had advanced to the second grade, Miss Stone's class on the second floor at the opposite end of the building from Miss Burglar. One day Miss Stone was teaching Health and Hygiene and was using graphic charts to explain the blood circulatory system. My seat was next to the radiator and I was feeling quite warm and vaguely uncomfortable looking at the charts and visualizing blood flowing around in my body. Suddenly, in my mind, I was at home in the kitchen and Mother had just dropped a dishpan, making a tremendous crash. The crash was my head hitting the radiator when I fell out of my seat. Coming back to reality, I saw Miss Stone and a half dozen awed kids staring down at me as I lay face up on the floor.

I don't know that this had anything to do with lack of adequate nutrition, but apparently Miss Stone thought it did. I remember her asking what I had eaten for breakfast and my reply, "Corn flakes and sweet milk."

It's true I was hungry a lot of times—I worried about the embarrassment it would cause if my stomach growled in class—but I thought that being very hungry before time to eat was normal. And that it was normal to wait until I got home to eat lunch. But a few days after the fainting incident Miss Stone gave me a meal ticket and told me to start eating lunch in the cafeteria. I recognized this as charity, which was anathema in my family. I was quite embarrassed. However, I went to the cafeteria and I still remember the mouth-watering aroma and the delicious taste of the soup with oyster crackers and the half pint of sweet milk. I presented my meal ticket with shame, sure that everyone around was watching me, and I stopped going to the cafeteria after two or three days.

I don't remember if it was before or after the fainting incident, but sometime while I was in the second grade an incident occurred which gave me much more reason for shame. I have kept it hidden in the darkest corner of my mind for the past seventy-two years. I know one day I must confess it before the Lord, so with the hope that practice may help me plead my case at that time, I'll relate it now.

We were at recess playing dodge ball when the bell rang and, for some reason, I lagged behind the other kids going back into the school. Hurrying to catch up, I saw a handkerchief lying on the ground. When I picked it up I discovered it had a coin tied in the corner. Elated at my good fortune, I stuffed it into my pocket.

Later that morning Miss Stone announced that one of the girls had lost her handkerchief with her lunch money and asked if anyone had found it. The blood drained from my body into the vicinity of my shoes, and my mind raced trying to decide what I should do. I felt that I had already convicted myself by pocketing the handkerchief instead of turning it in, and I would be totally mortified by revealing it now. So I kept silent.

During the following days I constantly fought my remorse and debated with my conscience. After all, I argued, the little girl's parents obviously had plenty of money to replace the dime she had lost, and the Bible said, "Finders keepers, losers weepers." But deep down I knew it was Billy Thomas who had said that, not the Bible. I suppose I spent the dime at Marino's candy store, but I suspect the candy tasted more bitter than sweet.

After about a year we could no longer afford the nice

house on 51st Street and we moved to a much more modest house on unpaved 52nd Street. We still had inside plumbing and there was an electric light bulb hanging from the ceiling in each room, but we could no longer pay an electric bill and began again to use kerosene lamps.

Billy Thomas and I continued to meet on our way to and from school, but I made a new friend, Reginald Revis, who lived across the street. Our happiest times involved building dams across the drainage ditch along the road to make muddy ponds when it rained. Also, we had one major project, which was to dig a mine into the high bank on his side of the road. We made a pretty impressive indentation, in which we buried tin foil from chewing gum wrappers to represent silver. Fortunately, we never got the excavation deep enough to cave in on us.

When I first heard Reginald Revis' name I thought it was so regal-sounding that he must be something like a prince. Familiarity soon taught me that he was just another scruffy little boy like me. Not so with Lawrence George and David Hadden. They were in my first grade class, but I saw them only at school. They wore nice clothes, brought fancy lunches to school and, with such richly resonant names, were obviously royalty. I wished I were more like them. I don't know that it was so much class envy as it was admiration, and an early recognition that many people were apparently "better" than I. This was an attitude that I recognized very early in my Dad: he treated everyone as if they were better than he. Not with subservience, but with respect. One of my earliest memories is hearing him defend Negroes in response to racial slurs about those who worked with him at the creosote plant. I think perhaps this humility is the thing that kept him from becoming bitter when misfortune kept pushing him back into poverty despite his hopes and hard work.

Work at the creosote plant dwindled down to nothing. We could no longer afford to rent at 52nd Street, so we moved again. Aunt Kate lived about a mile southwest in a house with a basement. I think Uncle Will was still at home at that time, so with Aunt Kate and our cousins, Floyd, Dora, and Odessa, there were five in the house occupying the main floor. Our family of nine moved into the basement. I remember very little about that situation, which apparently lasted only a short while.

About this time Floyd, aided by a sympathetic city employee, managed to purchase a house which had someway come into the possession of the city. This was located on Vinesville Avenue, two blocks from the house where we all lived. I'm not sure that it was done simultaneously, but Aunt Kate's family moved into the house on Vinesville Avenue and we moved into another house about a block away. I think the street was Court K.

One of the few things I remember about Court K was that we were again in a house without an inside bathroom. Even though this was in the city limits of Birmingham, we had a privy on an alley behind the house. About twice a week a sanitation wagon was driven through the alley and a crew of black men poured the waste from the outhouse into a tank on the wagon.

I also remember that Billy Thomas and I planted a garden in my backyard. Our main crop was popcorn, and it was with great excitement that we watched the sprouts break through the soil and grow in neat green rows. But I guess the rent came due, for we moved again when the plants were only four or five inches tall. This time two blocks, to Court I. Billy and I had a disagreement as to how we should handle our joint venture in agriculture.

Over his objections, I dug up the popcorn plants and re-planted them in my new back yard. Then Billy got mad because they died. Fortunately, disputes between eight-year-olds don't last long, so very shortly we were friends again.

I suggested in jest that we moved to Court I because the rent came due at Court K. Actually I'm quite sure we never moved to avoid paying the rent; if Daddy owed a debt he paid it. We moved to houses with lower rent so that he *could* pay it. But the house on Court I was a better house, with an inside bathroom and probably with higher rent. I suspect we moved there because Mother was expecting her ninth child and needed more decent living conditions. This house was nearly two miles from the creosote plant, but Daddy now went there mostly just to discuss their problems with the other laid-off workers and to pick up coke, burned coal, along the railroad track. We mixed this with regular coal or wood to burn in our cook stove and grates.

It's difficult for this generation to understand the depths of poverty that inundated a large portion of the population during this period of time. Jobs simply could not be found, not even chopping wood or doing menial chores. No one had the money to pay. There was no unemployment insurance or Social Security and the local "relief" agencies were under-funded and overwhelmed with requests for help. Aunt Kate could not be of help to us because her husband, Uncle Will Outlaw, had become sick and completely unable to work. Her son Floyd had been working since he was about fifteen at Pizitz Department store, and through diligence and dedication earned a reasonably good salary. He spent it unselfishly to support his mother, father and two sisters. In later years, he was also of help to us, but at that time there was hardly enough for his own family. Into this situation, July 5, 1931, the last of mother's children, Patsy Ruth, was born. Dr. Horner not being available, mother was taken to the Hillman Hospital in Birmingham for the birth. Photographs of mother around this time show a gaunt, overworked woman, who appears to be about sixty years old. She was forty-one.

In 1931 I was eight years old. I was well aware of our financial hardship, but having lived in austere circumstances most of my life, I was not particularly distressed. Billy Thomas lived nearby and we played together constantly when we were out of school. One of our major pastimes was playing marbles, and another, during the hot summer, was following the iceman as he delivered ice with a horse-drawn wagon. His customers displayed signs in their windows indicating the number of pounds of ice desired. The signs were printed with the number 25 on one side, and upside down below in the number 50. On the other side was the number 75 with the number 100 upside down below it. Thus the orientation of the sign could signify an order for 25, 50, 75 or 100 pounds and the iceman would cut off that amount, lift it with his tongs, and carry it in to the icebox. The ice pick always chipped off small pieces, which the iceman would pitch to a motley crew of kids trailing along on the dusty road.

I spent many hours, and ran many miles, playing with a homemade toy called a "click-and-wheel." This consisted of a solid steel rim (wheel) about eight inches in diameter and a handle made by bending a three-foot piece of wire to provide a handle at one end and square "U" shape at the other end to push the rim. It made a pleasant, metallic, singing sound and furnished imaginary transportation as I ran along the road and paths around the house.

Christmas, 1931, Santa brought me a scooter. It was not a sissy-colored, streamlined, reinvented version like kids have today; plain and simple tubular steel, it had fully exposed wheels large enough for any terrain. It was obviously "pre-owned." The scratches and rust did not bother me and I enjoyed it immensely. I was, however, somewhat disappointed that it did not—in the strict sense of the word—scoot. As long as I pushed with my foot, it moved. But when I stopped, it stopped. I discovered that the roller-bearing was missing from the front wheel. The wheel was two pieces of cup-shaped steel welded together on their concave sides. With the roller-bearing gone, the edges of the two pieces sat directly on the axle. Eventually it cut the axle in two. I replaced it repeatedly with twenty-penny nails, bent to hold them in place, but the friction quickly cut them, too. Finally the axle hole wallowed out to the point that the wheel just would not roll. So for transportation I went back to my "click-and-wheel."

Our gang consisted of Billy, three or four other boys, whose names I cannot remember, and me. We roved the neighborhood together searching for entertainment. Occasionally at the streetcar stop, we would see a man who showed us tricks; making coins disappear or pushing a cigarette up his nose and pulling it out his ear. To us, who had never seen a movie or a TV or a stage show, this was equivalent to a Broadway production. For me, it was the beginning of a lifelong fascination with magic.

Sometimes we would walk down a narrow dirt road that ran diagonally into Bessemer Boulevard to watch "Dummy." Where the two roads met, on a small triangular lot across from Aunt Kate's house, this old deaf and mute man lived in a one-room shack. There were all sorts of wild stories about him, probably none of them true, but everyone who passed stared with curiosity. Over a period of weeks we watched him labor to build, one board at a time, a ten-foot high fence to protect himself from the constant invasion of his privacy. Then we watched him laboriously saw off the top half of the fence on orders from the city because it exceeded the legal height. The other kids laughed in derision, but I felt a profound sympathy for the old man and wondered why in the world the city hadn't stopped him from building the fence too high in the first place.

Most of the kids wore short pants and no shirts. I was appalled at their immodesty and always wore a shirt. Partly, I suppose, this came from living in the country where the boys usually wore overalls and, following the example of their fathers, wore shirts to protect themselves from the sun. Also, I had become painfully conscious of my physique, I was tall for my age, extremely thin, and my shoulders sloped forward to create a "hollow chest." There was one stocky kid, the neighborhood bully, who taunted me about this unmercifully until, eventually, I decided I just wouldn't take it any longer. I would like to say that I beat him to a pulp, but the truth is I hit him one time, instinctively "pulling my punch" so it wouldn't hurt him, and immediately found myself on the ground with him sitting astride me pounding me with his fists. Though not physically hurt, I was thoroughly humiliated. The fact that I never became a famous prizefighter can be traced directly back to that incident.

I was not, to put it politely, a robust child. When I was about nine years old, mother took me to the clinic at Hillman Hospital for a check-up. Apparently they found no immediate problem, but they gave me the "Schick Test" for tuberculosis and instructions to return a few days later for the result. With seven other children to care for, two of them still babies, and possibly having trouble coming up with streetcar fare, mother decided to let me go for the test results by myself. I was a little apprehensive riding the streetcar downtown, then walking the three or four blocks to the hospital, but I did so without any problems. I checked in at the clinic and waited for my name to be called. The doctor was obviously surprised that I was by myself, and I sensed that he was somewhat chagrined. He looked at my arm to check the Schick Test, then said, "Go home and tell your mother you have TB."

I had heard a lot of talk about TB, sometimes in hushed tones, and knew it was a terrible disease. I had heard how children with the disease were sometimes sent to a "Fresh Air Camp" somewhere in Tennessee. I was in a state of anxiety all the way home, but at the same time began to anticipate the excitement of going away to a Fresh Air Camp.

I was also puzzled by the doctor's abrupt, almost angry way of telling me I had this dreaded disease. I suspect now that it was a rather cruel way of expressing his anger that I had been sent to the hospital alone. I don't remember returning to the hospital, but I'm sure Mother later talked with the doctor. And I'm sure I did not have TB. It was never mentioned again, and I didn't get to go to Fresh Air Camp.

In this present age, in which parents go with their grown children to register them in college, some may agree with the doctor who apparently thought my mother was negligent or even callous in sending a nine-year-old to a big city hospital alone. To the contrary, however, she looked after her brood like a setting hen. At that time, parents generally were not concerned about young children being alone in public from a safety viewpoint. And, as I can best reason it out, the day I went to the hospital the older children were all in school, Daddy was working, and Mother had no one to leave with the three younger girls, all under five. Also, if she had money enough for an extra carfare, she probably considered the fact that it was equivalent to two or three loaves of bread.

We were among the many "poor but proud" families of the Depression years. My father, particularly, was a firm believer that God helped those who helped themselves. As far as I know, there was only one time that we resorted to a breadline for food. Many thousands of people did. About a mile from where we lived there was a "relief" agency that regularly gave away bread on certain days each week. I suspect that Mrs. Prestridge, a relief volunteer who lived near us on Court I, had suggested to Mother that she take advantage of this practice. And I suspect the older children were too "proud" to go pick up the bread, for that chore fell to me and Margaret.

We walked down Bessemer Boulevard to the store building where the bread was being given away, and stood uneasily in the line making its way into the building. The arrangement inside was something like a cafeteria, with a man at the head of the counter asking each individual how many were in the family. Timidly Margaret told him "Ten," and we later giggled about his skeptical expression. But we progressed along the counter and they gave us enough loaves to fill two large sacks. On the way home we were delighted to discover one loaf was raisin bread, from which we took our transportation charge as we walked the uphill mile back home.

Shortly after this incident, with Mother and eight children to care for and no income, Daddy decided the only way we could live without charity was to return to the farm. The Old Home Place, then owned by Daddy's brother, Uncle Tom, was available if we could find some way to get there. Swallowing his pride, Daddy told the "relief" people if they could furnish us transportation we would not ask for anything else.

4
Back to the Old Home Place

The Red Cross furnished a truck and driver, who showed up about five o'clock one morning in March, 1932. W.T., Freeman, Daddy and the driver loaded our furniture onto the open-bed, stake body truck. The last piece was our sofa, which we called a "davenet," loaded in such a way that Margaret, Rebecca, W.T. and Freeman, ages 11, 13, 15 and 17, respectively, could sit facing toward the rear. Someone joked that they didn't care where they were going, they just wanted to see where they had been. Daddy, age 42, rode with the driver in the cab.

A tarpaulin was fastened over the load in case of rain during the nine-hour drive. The truck rolled gingerly down the curb into the street and pulled away, leaving Mother, the "three little ones" and me alone with the empty house. I remember that Mother said we had to leave the house clean and she had borrowed a broom from Aunt Kate to give it a final sweep. Whenever we moved she always insisted on scrubbing and cleaning the house we were leaving more than the one we moved into. "How would you like to move into a filthy house?" she'd say.

I figured nobody would be coming all the way to Tennessee to tell us we left a filthy house. Still I felt a sense of pride holding newspapers for her to sweep the dust and trash on, then carrying the wadded up papers and the broom down the hill to Aunt Kate's house on Vinesville

Avenue. We stayed with her two nights, but I don't know how she found places for us to sleep. Uncle Will, was in a hospital because of a "nervous breakdown," but our three cousins were at home. That is, they were there at night. During the day Dora and Odessa were in school and Floyd was at work, so we had the house pretty much to ourselves. Floyd was to play a very big part in my life later on, but about all I remember about him at that time was that he always had in his pocket a pack of "Lifesavers," which he would distribute to us kids.

Aunt Kate had a radio. We had gone to her house to listen to the radio before, but never had we got to listen so much as we did this time. I even learned to turn it on and off by myself. The main thing I remember listening to was the Hapi Wapi Club on WAPI. The leader of the club was an Indian chief named Hapi Wapi. I figured they hired him because of his name, which could be spelled with the station call letters.

Another thing I remember is turning the dining room electric light on and off. We'd had electric lights a few years before, but not since the Depression and we had never had a light like the one in Aunt Kate's dining room. We were fascinated by the fact that it could be turned on or off with a wall switch at the front door and another at the kitchen door. One of us would stand at each switch and I guess we turned that light on and off a thousand times. Aunt Kate probably would have guessed five thousand times.

We also played her piano, trying to pick out tunes with the keys or pumping the pedals to play tunes punched into a paper roll. Our playing always ended with Aunt Kate or Mother coming in and saying, "Why don't you go outside and play."

So Aunt Kate was probably relieved on the second

morning when we caught the streetcar right in front of her house to go to the train station downtown.

We had ridden the train to Birmingham some three years earlier, but I remembered nothing about it. So there was a first-time excitement as we waited for our train to be announced, then walked down the platform beside the tracks under a barrage of huffing, hissing and clanging from the trains, unintelligible announcements from the loud speakers, and the sounds of hurrying footsteps. The conductor helped us up the steps into the train and we found two seats facing each other. We heard the conductor yell "All aboar-r-r-d!" and through the window saw him swing himself up onto the steps as the train began chugging laboriously. We rolled along slowly until the city buildings began to disappear, and then settled into the rapid clickety-click rhythm we were to hear for the next several hours.

The most vivid memories I still retain from that trip are of a black porter with dazzling white teeth and friendly smile who came through the cars selling toys and trinkets. I was most fascinated by a glass pistol containing colorful candy beads, and a toy dog lying on a paddle who would stand up suddenly when you pulled a hidden string. Of course we didn't buy any of the trinkets, nor did we buy anything from the peddler who came through at intervals selling sandwiches, for Aunt Kate had provided us with a shoebox full of fried chicken and biscuits.

I also remember how the conductor came through the car a couple of times telling everyone to close the windows because we were approaching a tunnel. Even though they turned on the lights, it was rather frightening to go through the dark tunnel as the acrid smoke seeped in, burning our eyes and throats. The coal-burning engine belched clouds of soot and cinders, which drifted inside when the windows were open, causing everything to feel gritty and soiled. We had to change trains in Nashville, and had to spend several hours in a cavernous, domed waiting room. Announcements on the loudspeakers, and footsteps on the granite floor, bounced back and forth on the marble walls making everything sound amplified and unnatural. I remember in detail seeing a booth in the center of the room with a sign reading "Traveler's Aid." A nice lady came from behind the counter to talk with Mother, who was carrying Patsy Ruth and had me, Bertha and Bettie clustered around her feet. The lady left and returned with a baby bed for Patsy to sleep in the rest of the time we were there. I've had a soft spot in my heart for the Traveler's Aid organization ever since.

We sat a long time on a hard wood bench. Then a voice on the loudspeaker said "Dickson, Waverly, Memphis" and Mother said, "That's our train."

We got Patsy Ruth out of the bed and went down the steps and got on another train. This time it wasn't long before the conductor came to our seat and said, "Waverly, next stop."

The train started slowing down, the whistle blew two times, the bells started clanging, the steam hissed, and we came to a stop at a long wood platform. A colored man lifted up a trap door that covered the train's steel steps, swung down to the platform with our suitcase, and then helped us off.

Uncle Tom Forrest met us on the platform and with him was my cousin Ray. He was about my age and we kept eyeing each other but we didn't speak. I felt important because I had come from Birmingham on a train.

We started walking down the platform, and he said, "I meet the train most every day and sometimes I help them load the milk cans."

My feeling of importance went down considerably when I thought about him actually helping to load the trains. It took me a minute to think of it, then I said, "You ought to see the train station at Birmingham and Nashville."

I would have been all right if I'd stopped at Birmingham, but he said, "Oh, I've been to Nashville lots of times."

So all I could say was, "Well you ought to see the station at Birmingham." But saying it again like that sounded sort of weak.

We waited there on the platform while Uncle Tom went to get his car. Ray informed us that the car was a brand new 1933 Plymouth. We got in and Mother said, "This sure is a pretty new car. What kind is it?"

Uncle Tom said, "It's a 1933 Plymouth. I have to keep a good car carrying the mail. I swap my old car for a new one every year."

I didn't understand how in the world he could get anybody to swap him a new car for an old one, but I didn't say anything. I was too excited about riding in that car, I was disappointed when he drove into his yard and stopped after just a few blocks.

We spent the night at Aunt Betty's house, and we were greatly impressed by her shiny slick floors, the fancy dining room chairs and table, and her high, soft-looking beds. At supper we were overwhelmed by the taste and quantity of the food and by the variety of items on the table that nobody even bothered to pass; like jelly and jam and relish spread and pickles. I figured I knew why Ray was fat. But my other cousin Neal was almost as skinny as I was, and so was Uncle Tom. That was hard to figure out.

The next day, after Uncle Tom completed his RFD

mail route, he drove us out to the old home place, about seven miles out Clydeton Road, then left about one quarter mile on "the lane," a private road that led to the farm. The lane was so narrow that the trees on each side met overhead and their branches brushed Uncle Tom's car as he drove by, making it a mysterious and adventurous ride.

The lane ended at Big Richland Creek. Having been too young to remember when we lived there previously, I was impressed with the wide, swift-flowing, clear-water stream. On the other bank we saw Freeman, W.T., Rebecca and Margaret running down to meet us with Daddy, more dignified, walking behind. Beyond them I saw what I took to be the barn, and I asked impulsively, "Where's the house?"

Everybody laughed, and Mother said, "That *is* the house."

In 1887, Grandfather Stanfield had built that house as a modern replacement for the log cabin up in the hollow that his family had lived in prior to that time. My daddy was born in the new house in 1890. At that time, and for many years after, it was a picturesque homestead; a whitewashed house with a white picket fence, a large barn, a smokehouse, a chicken house, a buggy shed and a two-seat privy. Now almost every trace of whitewash was gone; the picket fence was gone and the privy was gone. The work buildings still existed but, neglected for years, looked dilapidated and forlorn.

It didn't take long to explore the house. It consisted of a single room on the left separated by an open hallway from three rooms, one behind the other, on the right. Three wide steps led up to the hallway, which we called "the porch," and a door opened into the rooms on each side. Those doors were only six feet high, which meant that Daddy had to duck a little to go in and out. The first room on the right we called the "front room" or the "living room." The next back we called the "dining room" and the last one was the kitchen. The room on the left was the "other room."

The chicken house was twenty-five feet or so behind the "other room." This was a low building, measuring about twenty by thirty feet, containing a "roost," a series of boards angling up from the floor to the ceiling, and a row of nests about four feet from the ground along each side.

The smokehouse was to the right of the kitchen, about thirty feet back against the foot of a hill, under a towering chestnut tree. It was about four feet off the ground. At hog-killing time, smoldering hickory-wood fires would be built under the house and the smoke would go through cracks in the floor to "cure" hams and bacon. I learned this through hearsay, since we never had a hog to kill.

The barn was one hundred feet or so to the right of the house on the other side of the spring branch. This was the most interesting of the buildings, partly because it had a loft half filled with peanut hay left by the farmer who had lived there the previous year. I spent a considerable amount of time scrounging through that hay for leftover peanuts. Some of the peanuts had begun to rot, so I learned the importance of eating one at a time; if a spoiled peanut was chewed up with some good ones it created a dilemma as to whether to swallow or spit. The farmer had also left a crib full of corn, some of which Mother used to make hominy, but most of which I chopped into short pieces to feed our cow.

The one other building, the buggy shed, was between the house and the creek. It was somewhat like a carport, with a shed on one side and a room for tools and feed on the other. An old automobile, which had no tires, no engine and no top, was parked under the shed. It did still have a front seat and steering wheel, which furnished hours of entertainment for my sisters and me. To that time, I had ridden in an automobile exactly three times. One of those times was when Uncle Tom picked us up at the train station and one was when he drove us out to the farm. The first occasion was when we lived at Harris Hooper's Place and I was four years old. Mother "caught a ride" with Mr. Bogus, who owned the Clydeton General Store and who drove to Waverly and back almost every day. We all sat on the front seat of this Model-T Ford. Recent rains had swollen a small stream that crossed Clydeton Road and when Mr. Bogus tried to drive across, we got stuck. I was frightened by the water rushing against and under the car, and became more and more agitated as he kept rocking the car trying to get out.

Finally I said, "Why don't we just turn around and go back?"

It seemed a reasonable question to me, but Mother and Mr. Bogus laughed as if it were a funny joke. I don't remember, but I assume someone pulled us out with a mule. This had nothing to do with my not riding in a car again for over four years, but perhaps will explain my tremendous interest in playing behind the steering wheel of that old car in the buggy shed.

In the isolated location of the Old Home Place, with primitive facilities and essentially no resources, all the children, down to and including me to some extent, became involved in the simple matter of surviving. But being only nine years old, play was still a big part of my life and a part that I remember most distinctly. No longer having Billy Thomas and gang, and no close neighbors, I made my own games or played with my sisters.

Margaret was eleven and Rebecca was thirteen, but in that unsophisticated time, children of these ages were still very much children. They "played house," drawing floor plans in the dirt and using sticks, stones and broken glass as furniture. I decided to open a store to serve the neighborhood. My brother Freeman, who was too old and mature to pay much attention to me normally, probably sensed my need for companionship. He built some shelves in the smokehouse so I could use it as my store. I stocked the shelves with empty tin cans, bottles, rocks and various sorts of grass and weeds to represent vegetables. But business was terrible. My sisters never seemed to find time to go to the store. Even though I'm not too proud of the accomplishment, at that time I invented the singing commercial. I strolled around their two-dimensional houses singing, "Tomorroo on Sundoo, you can't buy a thing." It didn't do much for my business, but ten years later Pepsi Cola pirated my idea with tremendous success.

When we first arrived, high grass and weeds were everywhere except close around the house where Daddy and my brothers had used a little curved-blade, one-hand sickle to cut them down. Young as I was, at that time I began to recognize the tremendous importance of tools, especially on the farm. As far as I know, the only tools we had were that sickle, a hoe, a pick, a shovel, a six-foot cross-cut saw, a double-bit chopping ax, a foot adz, and a "broad ax," which Daddy used for making railroad cross ties. I feel sure we also had a hammer, but apparently it was not available to me as I remember driving nails with a rock. I know we did not have a plow or a mule to pull it. Daddy, and sometimes Freeman and W.T. worked for the neighboring farmers in exchange for the use of a mule and plow.

To this day I wonder how Daddy was able to build a new outhouse with the available tools. The fact is, it was several days if not several weeks before he did so. Of much more importance was establishing a source of food, so he spent his time earning what little money he could for that purpose. Wisely, he first bought chickens, which could feed on grass, worms and berries from a big mulberry tree in the back yard, and which supplied eggs immediately and "fryers" within a few weeks. And someway he was able to buy a cow, which was probably the wisest investment he could make. It was an exciting time for us all when he returned from his long walk to Roscoe Turner's place and waded the creek leading "Jersey" behind. Though we lacked for other things, from then on we always had an ample supply of sweet milk, buttermilk and butter.

Looking after Jersey became my chore. She got water from the spring branch, which ran between the house and the barn. Most of her feed came from grazing in the unfenced pasture that lay beyond the barn, between the hills and Big Richland Creek. But we had to supplement her feed with corn and hay. In the late afternoon, at milking time, she would normally wander back to the barn on her own or when Mother summoned her by yelling "Soo-o-o-k Jersey." (Mother was accustomed to cows and spoke their language fluently.) But sometimes Jersey wandered so far down the creek that she either didn't hear Mother call or deliberately refused to respond. That's when I had to go "bring in the cow."

Thanks to my imagination, bringing in the cow was always an exciting adventure. The sage grass in the pasture near the house was higher than my head. So when I walked along one of the cow paths through it I could not see beyond the next turn in the path. Sometimes Indians or panthers or catamounts were lurking just around that turn. Or, if I got through the pasture safely, then I had to traverse a grove of trees that separated the pasture from the planting fields beyond. This was a favorite spot for Indians, catamounts and the like, too. So I always carried a stick. Luckily, I never had to use it except to prod Jersey. Otherwise the countryside would have been littered with dead Indians and catamounts.

When I located Jersey she would look at me in utter indifference or sometimes with obvious contempt in her big cow eyes. I would give her a piece of my mind for not coming in when she knew it was time for milking, and sometimes rap her rump lightly with my stick until she decided to humor me and walk leisurely home.

Occasionally, Jersey would eat wild onions. I despised the taste of her milk when this happened, and I let her know it in no uncertain terms. As I drove her home, I would use my stick a little more than necessary and say, "You git! And you better quit eat'n them dang onions. You know they make your milk taste terrible!" But I don't think she ever paid a bit of attention to what I said.

When I got Jersey to the barn I would use the ax to chop a few ears of corn into short pieces for her to munch while Mother milked. For some reason, which I assume was utter indolence (or udder ignorance) on the part of everyone else in the family, Mother was the only one of us who could milk. After milking she would take the pail of warm milk to the spring and set it in the cool water with a big rock on top of the bucket lid to hold it down.

The spring was our only source for refrigeration or for potable water. This was the most worrisome difference between living in Birmingham and here. We had to go to the spring, about one hundred and fifty yards up the hollow, for all water used for drinking or cooking. Fortunately, it was a big cold spring, gushing from under a huge rock in a high bank and sheltered by a massive beech tree. The path to the spring ran between a steep hill on the left and the spring branch, which flowed into Big Richland Creek. We got water from the branch, only fifty feet or so from the house, for bathing and washing clothes. Mother boiled the clothes in an iron pot over an outside fire and rinsed them in a galvanized wash tub. In winter, we carried that same tub to the kitchen and heated water on the cook stove for our occasional baths. In summer, we bathed in the creek.

5
The Creek

Countless springs emptied into Big Richland Creek keeping it quite cold, even in mid August when the atmospheric temperatures soared to three digits. But by the first day of summer we were going "swimming" at every opportunity. As suggested by the quotation marks, "swimming" is not a precisely accurate term. Except for Freeman and W.T. none of us could actually swim. We would wade gingerly into the water, shivering and shaking and yelping exclamations about the cold. Then by sheer will power push on until in water deep enough to submerge, but not too deep to touch bottom with our hands.

My first swimming occurred when I accidentally got beyond the intended depth and had to paddle furiously to keep my head from going under. Thus discovering that I actually could stay afloat, I learned to "dog paddle" and eventually to swim in a very rudimentary fashion on my side. I also learned to swim underwater and delighted in recovering white rocks thrown into the "Blue Hole," as we dubbed the ten-foot-deep water where the creek made a right-angle turn.

I swam in my pants or overalls, and the girls wore dresses. On one occasion when I was in my overalls a fish swam in at the bib and emerged through one leg, causing me to execute moves I wouldn't have thought possible.

And I remember another occasion when one of Rebecca's girl friends, perhaps a little older than she, came up out of the water with her dress clinging to her in a most interesting fashion. This was the first time that I can remember noticing such distinct physical differences between girls and boys. But I didn't give it a second thought—at that time.

During the summer I probably spent as much time in or on the creek as I did on dry land. From the Blue Hole the creek ran straight for about a hundred yards, getting shallower and broader to make the ford. Then it narrowed somewhat between two higher banks and this is where Daddy put in our foot log. Below the foot log the creek turned toward the left, shifting the water against the right bank, making the stream narrower and deeper and making it run swiftly. We quickly learned when walking the foot log that looking down at the rapid water could cause dizziness and loss of balance. Bettie Lois learned the hard way.

It was during the winter, and the creek was slightly swollen. Rebecca, Margaret, Bettie, and I were playing at the edge on our side just above the foot log. Bettie who was always a little bit daring or "headstrong," decided she would walk the foot log and, with the amazing swiftness of a five-year-old, proceeded to do so. We became aware of it only when we heard her scream followed by a loud splash. She had fallen on the down side and was going downstream toward the swifter, deeper water. Without taking time to remove her heavy winter coat, Rebecca rushed in, reaching her just in time. Their water-soaked winter clothing pulled her down but with a super strength created by the danger, she managed to make her way to shore with Bettie in her arms.

Hearing the screams and noise, W.T. came bounding

down to the creek, but by then all was well. Although immensely proud of Rebecca, I felt diminished and ashamed that I had not rushed into the creek to help. I consoled myself with the obvious fact that I would have done more harm than good. All of us "younger ones" adored Rebecca, and this act of heroism, following a similar act when we lived on Harris Hooper's Place, made us admire her even more.

Bathing in the creek, even on hot days, was uncomfortably cold. It was inconvenient to carry clean clothes to the creek and we got sand in our shoes and clothing when we dressed.

Searching for a better way, T came up with the idea of constructing a shower. His idea was to build a big wood box with a shower head (a tin can with holes in it) in the bottom and to mount it about eight feet high on the back of the smokehouse. The box would be filled with water by the rain, or by toting water from the spring branch. The sun would heat it, and we could then take a shower by standing under the box and pulling a string to release a stopper in the tin can. It sounded good to me.

Up the hollow a hundred yards or so beyond the spring was an abandoned sawmill with several stacks of lumber. These were rough oak planks, a full inch thick. Some of them were twelve inches wide and each one weighed approximately one ton. One at a time, over a period of several days, we carried planks from the sawmill to the smokehouse. T would carry the greater weight by holding the plank about one-third of its length from the front and I would trail along behind holding up the back end and asking incessant questions to which he gave purposely vague replies.

"How we goin' to saw straight enough to make a box with a cross-cut saw?"

"Who said I'm going to use a cross-cut saw?"

"Well, where we goin' to get a handsaw?"

"Don't you worry. I'll take care of it."

"How we goin' to get nails?"

"Don't worry. I'll take care of it. And if you're going to ride this board you can at least stop dragging your feet."

When we had toted enough boards, T borrowed a handsaw from Mr. Bryant, who lived across the creek at the end of the lane. We laid the boards across the steps of the smokehouse and my job was to sit on a board to hold it steady while T sawed and tried to ignore my questions.

"How we goin' to lift it when we got it done?" "How we goin' to fasten it to the smokehouse?" "How we goin' to keep it from leaking?"

Finally, in exasperation, he said, "If you ask one more question I'm going to wring your scrawny little neck!"

I was quiet for a while. Then I said, "How you goin' to catch me to do that?" And I instantly jumped off the steps and took off across the yard with him in hot pursuit. He caught me within a few steps, threw me to the ground, and tickled me, which was his favorite form of torture, until I begged for mercy.

Eventually, after a number of similar interruptions, the box was completed. Mother gave us a bunch of rags to tear into strips to "chink" the cracks, which T had purposely left between the boards because he knew they would swell when they got wet. T explained that we would put the box in the creek to soak and that the swelling then would keep it from leaking. The box, five feet square and two feet deep, was too heavy to lift, but by dragging and rolling we managed to get it down to the creek. We pushed it in. It promptly filled with water and sank.

The next day we bailed the water out of the box, but we never got the box out of the water. We could only guess how heavy it was; there probably wasn't a scale in the county of sufficient capacity to weigh it. Even T admitted there was no way to get it to the smokehouse, much less lift it eight feet high. He had done a perfect job of engineering the cracks and the caulking, so the box didn't leak a drop. It floated like a cork—or a battleship. So T cut a pole from a sapling and we got in the "shower" and pushed ourselves up to the Blue Hole then drifted back downstream. The girls stood on the bank looking at us and they laughed and said that was the funniest shower they ever saw. We decided we had been building a boat, but it continued to be called "The Shower." And T pretty much turned it over to me.

With a boat at my command, I spent even more time on the creek. On our side of the creek at the Blue Hole, the bank rose about eight feet above the normal surface of the water. From there downstream it tapered irregularly down to the water surface at the ford. Vegetation, mostly small willow trees, covered the bank. I used those trees to pull myself upstream to the Blue Hole, or pushed my way up with a pole, and then drifted leisurely back down to the ford. Sometimes I fished as I floated, using a cane pole, a line made by twisting two strands of thread together and a hook made with a bent pin. The bent pin was no good for larger fish, like bass, but using bits of biscuit for bait, I caught lots of perch and brim. I kept them on a willow stringer in the water so they would still be alive when I took them home, knowing Mother would tell me she couldn't cook them because she "didn't have any grease."

So I put the live fish in a hole of water in the spring branch. Downstream from the hole the water was very shallow, which kept the fish from swimming down to the creek. By the end of the summer that hole was like an aquarium, full of sun perch, black perch and brim.

I suspect Mother didn't want to fry my fish because they were too little. She was afraid somebody might get a bone stuck in his throat, and it was a seven-mile-walk to Dr. Horner's house. She didn't reject other forms of food from the creek. She managed to find plenty of grease in the lard bucket when T, Freeman or Daddy caught bass or catfish or bull frogs. I guess you wouldn't say they "caught" frogs; they "gigged" them. T made a gig by sticking an eight-inch piece of sharpened wire in the end of an old broomstick. It was thrown like a javelin when a frog on the creek bank was caught in the glare of the lantern on a dark night. When Mother started frying the frog's legs they would jump in the skillet, but by then it was too late.

I never tried to gig a frog, but one time I decided to gig a fish in my "aquarium" in the spring branch. At the bottom of the pool the water had washed out under the bank creating a natural hiding place for the fish. I plunged the gig into that cavity and pulled it out with three fish impaled on the wire! You probably think that's a whopper; but it's the gospel truth.

In the winter the creek changed its personality. The water didn't freeze, except sometimes along the edges, but it seemed brittle from the cold. Brown leaves accumulated in the eddies. T borrowed a bunch of steel traps from Mr. Bryant and we started trapping for muskrat and mink. We tied ears of corn on a string and soaked them in the spring branch until they swelled and soured. Then we set the traps in the eddies along the creek, hiding them under dead leaves, and put an ear of corn on the bank just beyond the trap as bait. We got up early to have time to "run the traps" every morning before we headed off to school and ran them again when we got home. It was an exciting adventure. Strangely, the getting up early, the cold and the discomfort added to the thrill.

We never caught a mink, but there were lots of muskrats and we caught several. T skinned them and stretched their pelts over boards, which he nailed in the sunlight on the side of the barn to cure. I believe Daddy had to take them to Waverly to sell them but they brought about fifty cents each. On one occasion, we caught a skunk. T chickened out on that one. Daddy skinned it and nailed its hide on the barn. Since the skunk hide brought a considerably higher price, Daddy was a hero in our eyes—but not in our noses. I remember that Mother was a little distraught about the whole thing. I think we went out of the trapping business at that point.

It was in the winter, usually, when the creek "got up." When this happened, our foot log was washed out and we were effectively marooned. Sometimes, when the water was not too high and relatively calm, we used The Shower as a ferry, pushing across with a pole. But when the waters were raging, the only access to the outside world was by way of the swinging bridge about a half mile upstream, halfway between our place and the Forrests'.

6
Hard Scrabble

Being only eleven, I was more concerned with play and "adventure" than the difficulties of keeping the family clothed and fed. But I was very much aware of those things as well.

Daddy, Freeman and W.T. worked whenever they could to earn a few dollars or, more often, in exchange for the use of a team and wagon or a mule and plow. This limited the amount of farming they could do because of lack of time and the fact that much of the work had to be done with a hoe. They cultivated a large garden between the house and the remnants of an apple orchard up toward the Forrests', and planted a few acres of sorghum and peanuts down the creek beyond the pasture. Once the garden was plowed and planted, Mother and us "younger ones" did the maintenance, hoeing, pulling weeds and picking bugs off the potato vines. Picking potato bugs became my specialty. I walked through the rows of vines, inspecting the tops and bottoms of the leaves, plucking the bugs and dropping them into a little coal oil in a tin can.

I also helped dig ginseng. This was a minor source of income, but decidedly worthwhile. Even in those days, ginseng roots, when dry, sold for about $16.00 per pound. More important to me, digging ginseng was fun. All four of "us men" dug ginseng, but probably T and I more than Daddy and Freeman. T was an expert at spotting the plants, which were almost impossible to find by someone without experience. Many other plants look somewhat like ginseng, but it has certain distinctive features—the shape of the leaves and the pattern of prongs—which give it an almost majestic look. Spotting a plant, deciding if it was mature enough to dig, then prying in from the loamy soil with a sharpened stick, was a thrilling experience, bringing such exclamation as, "Look at that—four prongs!" or, "Man! I'll bet that root alone will bring fifty cents!"

Often when we dug ginseng Daddy or T would go to a particular area where we would always find more than the average number of plants. They called it Daddy's "patch." Years before, when T was a small boy, Daddy planted hundreds of ginseng seeds in this spot and watched with increasing excitement as the plants came up year after year, adding "prongs" which indicated larger and larger roots. After five years he was ready to harvest his crop, which should have a value of several hundred dollars—in today's money several thousand dollars. But when he went to begin digging he found all the plants wilting and falling over. Alarmed, he dug up one plant after another and found that someone had already dug them, cut off the roots and then stuck the plants back in the soil. Daddy was literally sick. He had strong suspicions as to who the thief was, but had no proof and never made an accusation.

Daddy spent much of this time making cross ties. The farm consisted of about ninety acres, mostly wooded, so he had an ample supply of oak trees. He sawed down the towering trees with a two-man cross-cut saw, by himself when W.T. and Freeman were in school or working elsewhere. Then sawed them into the proper lengths and began work with his double-bit chopping ax, his monstrous, wide-blade "broad ax," and the foot adz from his days at the creosote plant in Birmingham.

When he had enough ties for a load, he drove a bartered wagon to the foot of the hill where he was working, used one of the mules to "snake" the ties down to the wagon, then upended the eight-foot ties and loaded them onto the wagon single handed. It was back-breaking work, which few men would have had the strength and determination to endure. Daddy took great pride in making perfect ties. I remember going with him once to the Clydeton General Store, where the ties were sold, and hearing the store owner say, "Charlie, they look like they were finished with a plane."

I didn't know what a plane was, but I knew it was a compliment by the way Daddy replied.

Counting the time it took to drive eight miles to Clydeton, Daddy netted only a few cents per hour for his labor. At that time, of course, a penny was worth as much as twelve pennies in 1999, so the amount of money Daddy made was not the best indication of our economic situation. The best indication of that was the number of things we possessed. It wasn't much.

The house had no closets. We didn't need any because the clothes that we were not wearing were hanging on nails on the backsides of the doors. I referred to "my shirt" and "my other shirt." If I talked about my pants and my overalls, the "s" on the end of the words didn't mean that I had more than one of each.

From the first warm day of spring until the first cold days of fall the younger ones, from me down, went barefooted. Even if old shoes were not worn out, our feet grew so much during the summer that we always needed shoes when it came time to go back to school. At $1.98 a pair, this was a major project, which was not always completed on time. I can remember walking to school and playing at recess with bare feet.

In addition to shoes for the young ones, there was the matter of new shoes and clothes for Freeman, W.T. and Rebecca. They would go to high school in Waverly and Rebecca, particularly, was concerned about "not having anything to wear." Margaret would be going to Trinity, but she was thirteen years old so she figured she needed new clothes, too. Bettie would be starting to school, but she got hand-me-downs from Margaret and Rebecca. Bee and Pat got hand-me-downs from Bettie, and they were pretty worn by then, but the "Little Ones" were too young for it to make much difference. Mother made all the girls' clothes, and sometimes she'd make new dresses even for the little ones. A lot of nights when we were gathered around the kitchen table, or even after we had gone to bed, we'd hear the pleasant whirring sound of her Singer sewing machine as she sewed by the light of the other lamp. There would be short bursts and pauses as she adjusted the cloth or went around a cuff, then she'd pump away on a long seam and the machine would speed up and hum along a mile a minute.

That machine was one of my favorite things; the sound of it and the way it smelled of wood and cloth and machine oil. I liked the feel of the varnished wood, the fancy wrought-iron legs and pedal, and the round rubber drive belt. Removing the drive belt, I would work the pedal and make the wheel go around so fast you could hardly see the spokes—when Mother wasn't around. There were two drawers on each side, and in the middle a long shallow drawer that tilted to open and close. The drawers were filled with all sorts of interesting things like spools of thread, a can of machine oil, scraps of cloth, thimbles, needles and pins. I guess I tilted that middle drawer open and closed a thousand times. And Mother told me to stop a thousand times.

Although Mother was sometimes hard pressed to prepare enough food for ten, we actually ate pretty well. The garden yielded enough vegetables to feed us through the summer, plus enough for Mother to can for the winter. The old apple orchard still had several good trees. I particularly remember the red-striped "June Apples" and the huge, green apples that we called, interchangeably, "Horse Apples" or "Pound Apples." We also had two or three peach trees—small "Indian" peaches which turned red when ripe and were delicious for eating or for making preserves. Just to the right of the house, we had what must have been the most prolific pear tree in the county, maybe in the whole great state of Tennessee. The pears were small, green and hard—not much good for eating raw. I think God made them that way purposely so we would not eat them all before mother could use them to make pear preserves for the winter.

And there were blackberries. Along fence rows and in patches scattered here and there, during the hottest days of summer, we picked blackberries. And during the hot summer nights we scratched chigger bites. Sometimes before going picking we wiped coal oil around our wrists and ankles to keep off the chiggers. It didn't work. Then we dabbed coal oil on the bites to make them stop itching. That didn't work either. But it was worth it all when Mother made rich, sweet blackberry cobbler and the most delicious blackberry jam this side of heaven. I wouldn't be surprised if God has her making that jam up there right now.

Although we had plenty of vegetables, berries and fruit, meat was another matter. The lack of refrigeration as well as the lack of money made meat a scarce item in our diet. The most frequent meat dish was corned beef hash, made with plenty of potatoes and gravy so one can would feed ten. We had canned salmon patties quite often, especially in our school lunches. And on special occasions we had fried chicken or chicken and dumplings. Except for "streak-of-lean" fatback, we very seldom had pork or beef. Usually breakfast was biscuits and gravy, biscuits and sorghum, or corned beef hash.

Occasionally we ate squirrel or rabbit. I remember the excitement of going squirrel hunting with T. We went early in the morning when the leaves were still wet so there would be no rustling to scare the squirrels. The best spot was near the spring, where the squirrels gathered nuts from the hickory trees and acorns from the oaks. T would send me to the far side of a tree to make a noise, and when a frightened squirrel fled to his side T would fell him with a blast from his twelve-gauge shotgun.

Once we built a rabbit trap. Because of our limited tools and materials, it was a unique design—a sort of pyramid-shaped box, constructed like a log cabin with one-inch cracks between the boards. We used palings from an old fence and nails salvaged from under the washpot where the boards in which they were originally used had been burned. It was a good combination: the palings were so soft that the burned nails could be driven through them quite well. We set the trap by propping up one end with three sticks arranged in such a way that a rabbit trying to take the bait would cause the box to fall. We were quite excited when we checked it later to find it had been tripped. Unfortunately, the paling boards were so rotted that the rabbit had gnawed off enough to squeeze through one of the cracks, leaving only telltale bit of fur.

Daddy had a surer method. I remember seeing him

go out in the field where he, Freeman and T had made piles of brush when they cleared the land. He shook the pile with his foot and a rabbit darted out. Daddy whistled. The rabbit stopped to see what that meant, and what it meant was that we had rabbit stew for supper that night.

Except for Mother's strength and perseverance (she called it "stick-to-it-tiveness") I don't know that we could have survived. Cooking for ten on a wood-burning stove was in itself almost a full time job, particularly since everything was prepared "from scratch." When washing, ironing, sewing, canning, milking and working in the garden were added to that she had a never-ending burden. Of course when they were not in school Rebecca and Margaret helped care for the young ones and I helped by working in the garden, and such things as bringing in stove wood, toting water, finding brush to burn under the wash pot, and fetching and feeding the cow.

7
School

Rebecca, W.T., and Freeman would be going to high school in Waverly. Sometime before school started Aunt Betty suggested to Mother that she let Rebecca move in with her, where she would be within walking distance of school. In exchange for room and board, she would help with the housework and taking care of Arbie Sue and Billy, who were two and five years old, respectively. (Ray was my age, and Neal was fourteen.)

Mother jumped at the opportunity, but Rebecca wanted no part of it. She accepted the arrangement reluctantly with the provision that she would spend the weekends at home. T and Freeman rode the bus to and from school, leaving very early in the morning and returning quite late in the afternoon. Margaret, Bettie and I went to Trinity School.

The community of Trinity consisted of Warren's Store, Trinity School and two farmhouses located about a half mile from our lane up Clydeton Road toward Waverly. At that point, Clydeton Road and Hall's Creek Road ran together diagonally, forming a "V." Warren's store was inside the point of the V, but about a hundred yards before the store there was a path on the left up a steep hill to Trinity School. This was a one-room, white frame building with four steps and a stoop at the front. Just inside the entrance on the right was a small table holding a five-gallon pail with a tin dipper. On each side of the door, mounted on the wall about five feet high, was a lunch shelf with nails in the wall beneath to serve as coat hangers. There were about thirty desks, each complete with ink well and a shelf beneath the writing surface to hold books.

Between the students' desks and the teacher's desk at the front were two benches facing each other, one on each side, where a class would sit to "recite." On the front wall was a blackboard. To its right was the "library" consisting of a bookcase with about twenty books, and to its left the exit door. A wood-burning stove in the center of the room furnished heat. Windows on each side furnished light. A path from the back door led to the outhouse, which was divided into two sections, one for girls and one for the boys.

I had completed three years of school in Birmingham, which was considered to have an excellent school system, with separate rooms for each class, and special teachers for writing, "art appreciation" and "music appreciation." But in the basic subjects of arithmetic, reading, spelling, history and geography I was somewhat behind my country classmates. Having to recite—read out loud and work math problems on the blackboard—made this immediately evident. But Mr. Ray* was an excellent teacher and the one-room school system was surprisingly effective, so I caught up quickly.

The average number of students per class was four. While one class recited, the others sat at their desks doing assigned work. We learned to concentrate on our own

---

*Ray Carter.

studies and disregard the reciting going on at the front of the room. Even so, I'm convinced we subconsciously absorbed some knowledge from the higher classes and I attribute some of my later academic success to the one-room school experience. The assigned work that we did at our desks was not a substitute for homework—our kerosene lamp could very well have been called a lamp of learning as we sat around it at the kitchen table almost every night.

Getting ready to go to school each morning was a mad rush. We had one Bible and one comb. Fortunately, W.T. and Freeman left before Margaret, Bettie and I, so it was only a three-way contest for the comb. That was not bad except when the comb got misplaced, which seemed to be about every other day. It wouldn't be on the dresser where it belonged and we would tear the house upside down looking for it. I don't know if Freeman, W.T., Bertha or Patsy was responsible, but I remember saying in exasperation that that comb didn't get up and crawl away by itself. Then after we got our hair combed Margaret and I would fight for the Bible. At school every morning after saying the pledge of allegiance and singing "My Country 'Tis of Thee" we had to recite a Bible verse, and we were supposed to learn a new verse every morning. We never seemed to prepare for this until about five minutes before time to start for school. We might get by repeating a verse occasionally, but Mr. Ray had a phenomenal memory and woe be unto you if he caught you doing this. It didn't take him long to rule out altogether "Jesus wept" and "God is love."

Rebecca never did get to where she liked living in Waverly. She said Arbie Sue was sweet, but Billy was the meanest kid she had ever seen, Ray and Neal teased her all the time, and she had to wash dishes and polish those shiny floors. She came home on the school bus every Friday evening. Long before she got there we would be standing out in the yard looking across the creek, and the minute we saw her coming through the lane we would run down to meet her at the foot log. Sometimes, because she was mad at Mother for making her live in town, she would be real grouchy at first. But after a while she would be out picking up chestnuts or playing hull gull* and enjoying being home.

One day shortly after school started Mother happened to see Freeman without his shirt on and saw with alarm that he had a tremendous bruised spot on his back. Under relentless questioning, Freeman finally confessed that he and T had "gone out for" football with the Waverly Tigers and he had got the bruise while practicing. Mother's response is not recorded, but suffice it to say that Freeman and T informed the coach the following day that they would not be playing football.

But six-foot teenagers were hard to come by, so a few days later the Tigers' coach made a sales call out on Big Richland Creek. He passionately proclaimed the value of football in building character, school pride, etc., and he assured Mother that injuries were almost unheard of because of the stringent rules and all the protective clothing and padding the players wore. Daddy took sides with Freeman and T, so Mother reluctantly consented "against her better judgment."

T was a freshman and never played on the varsity team. But Freeman, because of his six-foot-four-inch

---

*A guessing game played with chestnuts.

height, his speed and physical strength, became a valued player. Among our family photographs is one of the Waverly Tigers in 1933. Compared to the bulky armor worn by football players today, the shoulder pads and protective clothing of 1933 look remarkably flimsy. But neither T nor Freeman suffered any more injuries during the time they played.

There was one incident relating to their playing that caused some excitement. One evening Freeman was walking on a street in Waverly, I assume on his way to catch the school bus, when he passed out and fell to the street. Afterward he was okay, and his fainting was attributed simply to being hungry. Freeman and T took the same sort of lunch as we took to Trinity—two or three sandwiches made of biscuits with jam or fried eggs or salmon patties. This would have been sufficient except that they left for school so early in the morning and strenuous football practice burned a lot of calories.

At first we didn't play football at Trinity because we didn't have a ball. But after hearing T and Freeman talk about their playing, I scrounged a bunch of rags from mother and fabricated a "football" by sewing a large rag into a crude oval-shaped cover, stuffing it with the other rags and sewing up the opening. The result was so pitiful looking that I almost threw it in the creek, but I finally carried it to school and hid it at the edge of the school grounds. At recess I "accidentally" found it and exclaimed, "We could use this to play football!" There was some derision, but it was better than nothing. We played with it almost every day for a full season. No one ever knew I was the one who made it.

At the time, Mr. Ray seemed to me to be quite old, but I calculate now that he was probably in his early twenties. Some of the eighth-grade boys were not many years younger, and they were, to use the mildest applicable term, somewhat mischievous boys. For example, one Halloween night they cut two big trees and used them to blockade both doors to the schoolhouse. I remember quite well arriving the following morning and not being able to get in, but I don't remember if it accomplished the purpose of getting us a day off from school. Anyway, Mr. Ray faced a daunting task keeping his student body under control. But when he stood on the front stoop, rang his cowbell and announced "Books" all of us, including the big boys, took our seats and knew better than to misbehave in any way.

The only time I remember Mr. Ray's authority being challenged was one day when he was with a bunch of us boys eating our lunches in the school yard under a persimmon tree. We were talking about the fact that if you ate a green persimmon it would draw your mouth up so tight you'd have to eat through a straw. One of the eighth graders, Barthell Sykes, asked Mr. Ray if he would let us have the rest of the day off if he ate one. And Mr. Ray, thinking he was bluffing, said, "Sure."

Well, Barthell ate that persimmon. He couldn't talk very well with his mouth all "drawed up" but he said something like, "Aw 'ight, wus aw' go home!"

Everybody was laughing, including Mr. Ray, but he said, "Hold on, now. You knew I was just joking along with you. It's time for books."

But Barthell wasn't in a very good humor after eating that persimmon and he said something that sounded like, "You're just a dam wire."

Mr. Ray said, "What did you say!" And Barthell repeated it.

Mr. Ray said, "No pupil is going to talk to me like that!" And he got out his pocketknife and cut a long switch from a sapling. Then he said, "John C., hold my coat."

Barthell held up his fists like he was going to fight, but Mr. Ray grabbed him by one shoulder, spun him around and gave him three or four whacks with the switch. Then he threw the switch down, took his coat from me, and said, "It's books now. Go in and take your seats."

Barthell never did like me after that because I held the teacher's coat. I felt sort of bad about it. Mr. Ray *did* say he would let us go home. But what else could I do?

Barthell's brother, Elton, already disliked me because Mr. Ray selected me instead of him to be Santa Claus in our Christmas play. We practiced the play at school for several weeks, then presented it the week before Christmas at Bethlehem Church, which was about a quarter mile toward Waverly on Clydeton Road. They lit up the church auditorium with a lot of lamps and lanterns, and they had a big Christmas tree with real candles and presents for all the children in the neighborhood. The audience filled the auditorium, which held about seventy-five people.

This was my first introduction to show business, and I was enthralled. Margaret was in the play, too, and she, like me, still remembers our opening song:

We welcome you, we welcome you;
Though we are young our words are true.
Just settle down and be impressed;
You listen, we will do the rest.

I played a character who, in the play, "played Santa Claus." Elton Sykes was indignant that he was not chosen for the part because he was quite chubby, an ideal

Santa Claus, and I thin as a reed. I wore a red jacket, a red cap and a fake beard, but no pillow. The laughter was uproarious when I made my appearance in that garb.

In the other part of my role I was supposed to be *intentionally* funny. I had a long, funny speech, most of which I was supposed to read from a letter taken from my coat pocket. I was horrified when I started to read to find that the page was blank. Fortunately, I had rehearsed so much that I had almost memorized the letter. By simply pretending to read I managed to stumble through. I don't know how he could have done it, but I think Elton Sykes someway switched the letter for that blank piece of paper. The fact that I did not become a renowned stage actor can be traced directly back to that incident.

Mr. Ray had a present for every pupil under the Christmas tree. Mine was a book about a deer. I remember it brought tears to my eyes when I read it. I'm not sure, but I think it was "Bambi." I am sure Mr. Ray gave me a book because he knew I had read just about every book in the school "library."

My presents at home were a little tin box of watercolors and a homemade shirt. I was completely surprised and delighted with the watercolors. But, despite our almost universal poverty, my schoolmates were like children of every age, they considered certain things "tacky." And one of those things was wearing a homemade shirt. I remember being relieved that no one could tell that mine was not "store bought."

One day Mr. Ray had to be absent from school and, because my sister, Margaret, was in the eighth grade and fourteen years old, he made her teacher for the day. She didn't have quite the control over the students that Mr. Ray had. There was another occasion when Mr. Ray's sister filled in for him so I'm not sure whether it was then or when Margaret "taught," but I remember the older boys engaging in some very funny horseplay involving the water bucket. One raised his hand and asked if he could get a drink of water. He made a big to-do going to the water bucket, drank a bit of water then, because the rule was that you did not put water back into the bucket, opened the door and threw out the water remaining in the dipper. Then another boy went through the same routine. Then another, until everybody was laughing and talking. I don't remember how the substituting teacher restored order—if she did.

I didn't mind going to school too much, but I was always ready when four o'clock came and school was out for the day. I beat everybody getting down the hill to the highway. Then, while the other kids meandered along, the younger ones playing and the older ones flirting with the girls, I hurried on down to Mr. Bryant's house, just across the highway from The Lane. If he had not already taken in the mail and the newspaper from his mailbox I would do so. In any case, I would walk back to his hundred-year-old log house and knock on the door. He or Miss Annie would say, "Come in," and I would go into the room where they sat in rocking chairs before a gigantic fireplace.

They would say, "How are you, John C?" And I would say "Fine," and give Mr. Bryant the newspaper. He would give me back the funny paper and we would sit there and read, usually without saying another word.

I enjoyed those funny papers! Especially on Monday, when we got the Sunday paper. In those days, the funny papers were truly funny: The Katzenjammer Kids, Mutt and Jeff, Li'l Orphan Annie, Out Our Way and Bringing up Father (Maggie and Jiggs).

Miss Annie read the paper, too. But she had a difficult time of it because she moved her head back and forth constantly. Mother told us that Miss Annie had suffered with this affliction all her life, and that it was particularly tragic because she was such a pleasant, intelligent lady. Among our family photographs is one of mother with a group of young ladies, including Miss Annie, and her face is blurred beyond recognition because of her moving her head. I liked Miss Annie very much, and I use to pray that she could stop moving her head all the time. But I guess she never did until she died.

Mr. Bryant, with his white hair, white beard and white, bushy eyebrows looked almost as old as his house. I was fascinated by his walking stick, which was like the limb of a tree with all the bark peeled off. I thought it looked like Mr. Bryant; gnarled and knotty and slightly crooked, but very strong. I marveled at the way that old man could lift a huge log to put in his five-foot-wide fireplace.

One time Melvin Sykes and I were playing in the branch that ran across the field in front of Mr. Bryant's house, trying to catch minnows for fish bait. He was walking nearby and asked if we needed help. Then he walked along the branch with us and used that crooked walking stick to point out the minnows. He could see them before we did despite his age, and he didn't even wear glasses.

8
Danger

The two greatest dangers we faced in our day-to-day living were drowning and snakebite. Except for the time when Bettie fell off the foot log, no one ever came close to drowning, but we had several near misses involving snakes. As we approached the creek, on the left side of the lane just before a grove of beech trees there was a thick growth of cane, which we called the "cane brake." Once as I passed this point on my way home I heard the unmistakable, terrifying rattle of a diamond-back rattlesnake. I jumped sideways about ten feet and ran on home yelling for T. He grabbed his shotgun and led the way back to kill that snake. When we couldn't find it T became skeptical and said I must have flushed a covey of birds and it sounded like a rattlesnake. I was indignant.

"I've flushed them old birds a thousand times," I exclaimed. (I was inclined to use a little hyperbole with T because he was guilty of a little of that, himself). "I know a dang rattlesnake when I hear one!"

A more perilous occasion occurred once when Mother went to the spring. She dipped a bucket of water and had straightened up to leave when she heard the terrifying sound. She froze in place, which is sometimes the best thing to do, but the snake had already coiled and sprang toward her. Fortunately it had bad eyesight and it hit a twig, which deflected it enough to miss her. She jumped across the spring branch and ran all the way home. After our alarm had calmed, I joked that for a while we had running water. But I believe I'm the only one who thought it was funny. Definitely not funny was the time when Patsy, less than four years old, went into the hen house to check the nests for eggs, which she loved to do. She came running out crying "Snake! Snake!"

Mother heard her and yelled for T. Again he snatched up his shotgun and rushed to the hen house. We heard the blast of the shotgun, and a few seconds later T came out with a six-foot rattlesnake draped over the end of the gun barrel.

He skinned that snake with the idea of making a belt. But apparently curing a snake hide involves something more than hanging it over a clothesline. After a few days Mother made him bury it to get rid of the odor and the swarming of green flies.

Digging ginseng and picking blackberries exposed us to the constant danger of snakes, chiggers and ticks. Chigger bites were a great irritation, but not dangerous. We frequently had to pull ticks from our bodies and thought the only danger was infection in the bitten spot. So sometimes we touched the tick with a lit cigarette to make it loosen its grip to reduce the laceration. But we knew nothing about the life-threatening danger of Lyme disease caused by ticks. Maybe "Lyme" hadn't invented it, yet.

Another danger, to me, was W.T. But I guess I brought it on myself. Like the time we went to dig ginseng and I over used my favorite cuss word, dadgum. I complained about the dadgum sweat bees, the dadgum bushes that kept hitting me in the face, and the dadgum rotten logs we had to keep stepping over. I exclaimed about the size of the dadgum ginseng then, on the way home, "These dadgum saw briars are 'bout to tear my dadgum feet up. I should have worn my dadgum shoes."

Finally, T exploded. "If you say 'dadgum" one more time I'm going to skin you like a snake!"

By then, we were at the spring branch and I stayed quiet while we stooped to wash off the ginseng roots. Then I said, "T, if it was Dad's birthday and you were going to give him a present, would you give Dad gum?"

I was off like a shot, but he was right behind me. As usual, I ended up on the ground with him sitting astride me, tickling me until I was gasping for breath.

When Daddy was in the woods making cross ties he was exposed to all the normal hazards plus the danger of falling trees and other accidents inherent in the work itself. One afternoon on the way home from school we were made aware by everyone we saw that one of those accidents had occurred. Considering the fact that there were only two or three telephones in the neighborhood, it was amazing how quickly the news had spread.

While making ties, Daddy had cut his leg very severely. He was near the top of a hill behind our house. Realizing that he was losing blood rapidly, Daddy yelled as loud as he could, "Call the doctor! I've cut my leg!"

Mother did not hear him because she was in the lane on her way to check the mailbox. Fortunately, however, someone on Clydeton Road heard the sound, which went over her head. They found a telephone and called the doctor—Doctor Horner, I assume.

Meanwhile, with his overalls leg soaked and his shoe filled with blood, Daddy made his way to the vacant house. He found the shotgun and fired several shots, not knowing if his shout had been heard.

I don't know the details, but Daddy was taken to

Waverly for treatment and stayed with Aunt Betty while he recuperated. After several days, Uncle Tom drove him home. When we heard the car coming through the lane we all rushed down to the creek to meet him. Daddy was on crutches and there was some consternation as to how he could walk the foot log to cross the creek. Excited at the prospect of being the "hero," I yelled to Daddy, "I'll bring you across in the Shower!"

I pushed my ship into the creek and poled it across and several yards upstream. Daddy got in, somewhat uneasily and I, feeling like Washington crossing the Delaware, expertly pushed across the current as we drifted downstream, then proudly landed on the home shore.

I had thought that Daddy had cut himself with his wicked looking "broad ax." But actually it was with his regular chopping ax, which glanced off an unseen knot. He was fortunate that it did not break his shinbone and that he did not die from loss of blood.

With no refrigeration and rudimentary sanitation facilities, eating lunches wrapped in newspapers and stored several hours in a warm room, all drinking from the same dipper at home and at school, we were constantly exposed to the danger of food poisoning and infectious diseases. Perhaps this constant exposure built powerful resistance for we were seldom sick. Also, nothing organic on our clothes and bed sheets could have survived the scrubbing and boiling and the Octagon soap that mother used when she washed. And despite the lack of bathing facilities, we kept reasonably clean. W. T. was especially conscious of good hygiene (that's what led to the construction of the "shower") and he taught me the importance of thorough bathing and brushing teeth.

We didn't have toothbrushes, so we made a sort of brush by chewing the end of a willow twig. We used salt and soda as a substitute for toothpaste. Rebecca was so obsessed with brushing her teeth that she was almost a fanatic—even going to the extent of brushing them with Octagon soap. Of course she was fifteen years old, very pretty, and very conscious of her appearance. (I believe she was voted "the prettiest girl" at Waverly High School.)

A common problem in those days, especially among school children, was scabies—which we called the seven-year itch. One day Mother noticed me scratching between my fingers. She checked my hands and said, "Oh, my! You've got the itch."

I was horrified, calculating that I would be scratching until I was nineteen years old. Some of the others showed symptoms, too, so Mother had all of us take a hot bath and proceeded with the only known treatment, which was the all-over application of sulfur and sorghum molasses. It was uncomfortably sticky and gritty, and smelled terrible. But at least it got us out of a few days of school.

When they lived in the Old Home Place after they were first married Mother insisted that Daddy put in a small window, about eighteen inches square, in the living room to the left of the fireplace. This was so she could look out toward the barn, the pasture and the path to the spring. The "other room," where Freeman, T, and I slept, had a window on each side. Except for that, each room had only one window, measuring about two feet wide and four feet high. So the interior was rather dark even on a bright day. This was probably the reason for another embarrassing episode regarding sanitation: We discovered that we had bedbugs. When this happened, Mother flew into a frenzy of activity. Under her orders, we stripped every bed. Sheets and washable covers went into the iron wash pot and all the other covers and mattresses were put on boards outside and exposed to the sunlight for a full day. We dipped rags in coal oil and wiped down the bed rails, springs and every seam and crevice in the mattresses. We were accustomed to the smell of coal oil, so it didn't bother us particularly, and I don't think we ever had the problem of bedbugs again.

9
Interlude

Right after Christmas in 1933 our cousin, Floyd, took a train to Waverly and Uncle Tom drove him out to Big Richland Creek. Floyd was five years older than Freeman and had been close to our family all his life. He lived his early years on the Tennessee River in Danville, Tennessee, where his daddy, Will Outlaw, ran a "General Store." Danville was mentioned once in Ripley's *Believe It or Not* newspaper column because the signs of the three main merchants read, "Outlaw," "Gamble" and "Steele." At that same time in McElwain, another small Tennessee town, Aunt Kate's father (my Grandfather John Fry) was one of three merchants whose signs read, "Fry," "Ham" and "Brown." If you don't find that interesting, just skip this paragraph.

Floyd saved my life. He didn't know he did and I, being only a baby at the time, didn't know it either. But I came to the conclusion that he did when Mother related this story: Mother was visiting Aunt Kate and she had me with her. I assume Freeman, W.T., Rebecca and Margaret were also along since they were all less than ten years old, but apparently Daddy was not. I "came down" with a terrible case of whooping cough, which became so bad that I could hardly breathe and they thought I was dying. There was no doctor in Danville, but they learned that a doctor would be on the train scheduled to pass through

Danville that evening. The train would stop only if there were passengers getting off at Danville, or if it was flagged down. Floyd went to the station, had the train stopped, found the doctor and explained my predicament. The train was delayed while the doctor went to see me. The weather was cold, and I was in a room closed up tight to keep me warm. The doctor immediately had the doors and windows opened wide and, with an increased source of oxygen, I began to improve almost immediately.

I didn't know this story when Floyd visited us in 1933, but all of us were delighted with his visit. He was always pleasant and cheerful, and he had a way of making everybody he talked with feel cared-for and important. His father was hospitalized, and Floyd had been working to provide for his family since he was fourteen. Having no brothers and no father at home, he probably needed male companionship. Freeman and W.T. were at ages where their own interests occupied their time, which may be why Floyd devoted a great deal of time to me. He had an innate inclination to help those in need and apparently he felt a particular compassion for me. With my skinny limbs, my sloped shoulders and my flat chest, I suppose I was a somewhat pathetic-looking child. Also, because Floyd had always lived in comparative luxury, I'm sure he found our meager home distressing.

Whatever the reason, Floyd suggested that he take me back to Birmingham for a vacation while school was out and send me back on the train. Surprisingly, Mother and Daddy agreed. First he planned to go to McKinnon (near Danville) to visit his father's sisters, Aunt Mattie and Aunt Polly. Daddy arranged for "Goose" Ellison to drive us to McKinnon in his Model-A Ford. This was the fourth or fifth time I had ridden in an automobile, and the first time for more than five or ten miles. It was about thirty miles to McKinnon on dirt roads which swerved first one way then the other around those Tennessee hills. There was no heater in the car, so it was a cold trip, but I enjoyed the ride and the unfamiliar scenery—particularly the high clay banks where the road had been cut into the hills.

At McKinnon, we stopped briefly in front of Aunt Polly's house while Floyd went to the door to ask how to get to Aunt Mattie's. A girl about my age came to the door with Aunt Polly and stood with her arms folded across her chest, looking with curiosity at the car. I was smitten by her short blonde hair, her cute sailor-type blouse and the mature way she stood by as Floyd and Aunt Polly talked.

We went on around another hill to Aunt Mattie's house, where we stayed two days. Aunt Mattie was one of those people whose main interest in life seemed to be apologizing for being there. But she was very sweet and pleasant and, most important, a good cook.

I enjoyed the two-day visit, especially when we went to visit Aunt Polly and I got to meet the girl with the short blonde hair, Floyd's cousin, Oretta. Floyd did his best to develop a "relationship" between us, although the word had not yet been invented. But she wasn't exactly overwhelmed. In fact, I don't think she was whelmed at all. I think she was too mature for me. Anyway, I was still carrying the torch for my first love, Jeannette, from Miss Burglar's first grade. I still remembered the electric shock when we were learning a Dutch folk dance in Gym and I touched her hands to the lyrics, "With our hands, we clap, clap, clap." (There was also something about wooden shoes, but the electricity obliterated everything except the bit about the hands.) I'm still carrying that torch even though it's been seventy-two years since the last time I saw Jeannette: Mother and I were walking back home after going to the Health Clinic in Central Park. We passed Jeannette playing in her yard with some other kids and *she spoke to me.* My mind raced to come up with the right response. I pointed to my open mouth and said, "I got my throat painted."

I immediately knew Jeannette was not overly impressed. I had that feeling a number of times after making comments of similar brilliance to Oretta.

We rode the train from McKinnon to Birmingham, and Floyd saw to it that I had a great time for about four days. He took me to the first movie I ever saw; a silent film called, "Lady Bonnett." It was not really silent; there was no talking, but there was music. I remember because the music got very fast in the funniest part where two men, policemen I believe, were chasing Lady Bonnett and she ran into a ladies' rest room. The men didn't see the sign and ran in after her, then came out with their faces fiery red. It was a black and white film, but there was no doubt their faces were red because of the way they acted.

When it was time to go home, Floyd put me on the L & N train for Nashville. I was almost twelve years old then, and I had changed trains in Nashville once before, so I didn't have any trouble at all. On the way to Waverly, another young boy traveling by himself sat with me. I was fascinated when he pointed out a farm just outside of Nashville where they raised Shetland ponies. He went on to Memphis, I think. But I got off at Waverly. Ray met me at the railroad station and while we were walking to Aunt Betty's house he told me about his latest project, which was picking up scrap metal to sell. I figured to top him by telling about Lady Bonnett, but he had seen several movies already. I never could seem to get ahead of Ray.

10
W.T.'s Christmas

Sometime during the winter of 1934, Daddy learned that the creosote plant in Birmingham had reopened, that he could get his old job back and also a job for Freeman. Since we were "barely making it" on the farm, he accepted the opportunity. Freeman dropped out of school and they rode a bus to Birmingham. I'm not sure whether they stayed with Aunt Kate or found a boarding house but, in any event, they moved to Birmingham while the rest of us stayed at the Old Home Place.

A few days before Christmas, W.T. decided that we should have a Christmas tree. I was only eleven, so T, who would be eighteen on Christmas Day, was the man of the house and assumed the responsibility for important decisions such as putting up a tree. He took the double-bit ax from the chopping block and, with me tagging behind, went up the path to the spring, then into the woods on the steep hill to the right where we had been squirrel hunting a few days before. It was also the spot where, about a month earlier, we had cut down a towering oak tree for firewood; a tree that Daddy later said, with some chagrin, would have made six good cross ties. We found a Christmasy pine and T felled it with a few licks with the ax.

With T dragging the tree and me following importantly behind with the ax on my shoulder, we started the trek back home. Next to the tall oaks, the pine had looked quite small, but T was grunting and, despite the cold, breaking into a sweat by the time we got it home. He drug it around the house to the entrance to the "dining room." The house was shaped like a reversed "L" with three rooms one behind the other on the long part of the "L." The dining room was the middle of those three rooms, and the entrance was inside the "L." The floor was about three feet above the ground, but there were no steps. Whether the steps had rotted away or simply had never been built was a matter of conjecture. It was of little consequence because we seldom used that entrance anyway. However, this was a convenient place for us to carry the Christmas tree into the house.

At that point we made an interesting discovery; the ceiling was something less than eight feet high and our tree was something more than twelve feet long. After some discussion we decided it would be easier to cut off the tree than to raise the ceiling, so T wielded the ax again. As I remember, it took two or three cuts, but he finally got the tree short enough to fit. Also, someway, we managed to construct a stand to hold it in an upright position.

We left it to Mother and the girls to decorate. Mother stirred up the fire in the cook stove, put some popcorn in an iron skillet and covered it with a lid. Soon a pleasant popping sound mingled with the metallic sound of the skillet as she slid it back and forth on the stove lid, and the house was filled with the delicious smell of popping corn. Rebecca and Margaret found red berries, which we called "haws," on bushes near the house and used a needle and thread to make long strings of berries and popcorn. Apparently we had brought colored paper from school because they also made paper chains, using paste made from flour. There were no candles and no lights, but to us it was a beautiful sight.

A few days later, in the afternoon of Christmas Eve, T announced that he was going to the store. I don't remember that he asked me to go along, but that was not necessary: in those days practically everywhere T went I was by his side or lagging a few steps behind. So I followed him across the foot log, through the lane and then right toward Warren's Store on the gravel road.

During the twenty-minute walk, some version of the following conversation was repeated approximately twenty times:

"What you going to the store for?"

"What does anybody go to the store for; to buy something."

"How you going to buy anything when you ain't got any money?"

"Who said I don't have any money?"

"I know dang well you ain't got any money!"

"We'll see."

"Sure 'nuff, T, where did you get any money?"

"Did I say I had any money?"

"Did Mother give it to you?"

"Now where would Mother get any money?"

"Well, how the hang are you going to buy anything when you ain't got any money?"

Warren's store was not a big, fancy place like the general store in Clydeton. It was just one room about the size of our front room and dining room put together, with a porch and a door at the front and a door without a porch at the back. It had a fire going in a big potbelly stove, so it felt pleasantly warm when we walked in. And it made you hungry to smell the crackers and cheese and coffee and stuff.

Mr. Warren said, "How're you, W.T.?" and "How're you, John C.?" and asked T if we'd heard from Charlie. And they said it sure is cold and things like that.

Then T said, "Mr. Warren, I was wondering if I could put a few things on the bill?"

My mouth fell open in astonishment. So that was it!

Mr. Warren said, "Sure."

Then he started filling up paper sacks as T told him he wanted a dozen oranges, a dozen apples, a pound of Brazil nuts (which we quite innocently called "nigger toes") and a whole bunch of other stuff like that. I was immensely proud of the nonchalant way T ordered things as if he did that sort of thing every day. I wondered how he was going to pay for it, but I knew he sometimes worked for neighboring farmers, plowing, picking up rocks and clearing fields. So that must be what he had in mind.

While Mr. Warren got the things T ordered, I was eagerly studying the bins of candy and chewing gum in the glass case in the middle of the long counter. I was particularly fascinated by a pack of gum that had a "prize" attached to it. The prize was an artificial flower with a rubber tube leading to a hollow rubber ball. I saw the possibilities at once. And I also had a sudden impulse to buy T a Christmas gift. I was much too timid to ask Mr. Warren direct, but I got T's attention and told him I wanted to buy the gum. He asked Mr. Warren how much it was. Mr. Warren said three cents and, excited that it was not more, I asked, "Does that include the prize?"

When he assured me the prize was included, I told T I wanted to buy it. He said, "Okay," then in a mature tone to Mr. Warren, "That'll make a nice present for one of the kids."

Indignantly, in my high-pitched eleven-year-old voice I blurted out, "I'm buying it for you!"

Mr. Warren laughed. T turned beet red and, seeing that he was embarrassed, I felt my face turning red, too. I was relieved when Mr. Warren completed tallying the bill and we left. Outside, my embarrassment changed to excitement as T explained that we were going to slip the fruit and stuff into the house without Mother and the girls seeing us. However, I couldn't figure out how we were going to do that, so began my usual doubting questions. T egged me on with his "that's-for-me-to-know-and-you-to-find-out" replies.

But his plan began to emerge when we reached the Ellison place and he turned left on the lane that led to the swinging bridge. The bridge was about halfway between our place and the Forrests', the only other farm on our side of the creek. It had been built by our granddaddy and the Forrests to provide a way across when the creek was "up" and the foot logs were washed out. Like our house, it had been built some fifty years ago and was badly in need of repair. Basically, it consisted of four cables about twelve feet above the surface of the creek, held together with other cables and floored with boards. It ran from a high rock bluff on our side of the creek to a wood tower on the other side. T had told me that each of the main cables was anchored to a dead man buried six feet deep. I found this fascinating but gruesome, and every time we crossed the bridge I would start asking T if the cable were really, sure 'nuff, held down by dead men. He never did explain that a "deadman" is a buried log.

A lot of the boards had rotted away, which made crossing the bridge a scary experience when the creek was up and you could see the rushing water twelve feet below. But on this occasion the creek was shallow, the water ran gently, and we had no trouble crossing even with each of us carrying two full paper bags.

Foreseeing a problem when we reached the house, I said, "How the hang are we going to get the bags into the house without Mother and the girls seeing us?"

T said, "They can't see when they're asleep."

After a few more persistent questions and evasive responses, T explained that we were going to hide the bags along the way and come back for them after dark. About halfway to the house, at a spot where the creek bank was quite high, there was a depression almost deep enough to be called a cave. We hid the groceries there and proceeded on home. It was not unusual for us to wander off down the creek or into the woods for a few hours, so no one had noticed our absence.

At first dark, we went to the room we slept in, the "other" room, the one on the left. There was no heat in that room, so we went to bed to keep warm. However, we did not take off our clothes and as soon as we surmised that Mother and the girls had gone to bed, we sneaked out the door and up the familiar path toward the Forrests'.

I don't remember that it was unusually dark, but I remember that I graciously let T lead the way. We found our bags as we had left them in the cave, and we also found that the burden of the bags and the darkness made it a little more difficult to negotiate the trail going back. But the sense of adventure and excitement made it easy to endure the cold and the discomfort, even when we slipped and slid down the high bank of the dry spring branch that separated the Forrests' farm from ours.

When we got near the house, we started talking in whispers and stealthily made our way to the dining room door. We opened the door just enough to slip the bags in under the tree, then went to bed. As the warmth accumulated under the covers, I lay awake, still excited from our escapade, imagining how surprised Mother and the girls would be in the morning. I thought about the fun T would have squirting people with the trick flower, and wondered if he might lend it to me to take to school. I could hear myself asking Barthel Sykes to smell the flower, but reconsidered when I remember that he once threatened to push in my face and was undoubtedly capable of doing so. Lying next to me, T was beginning to breathe heavily, and shortly, I also, was asleep.

I don't remember anything at all about the reaction of the girls, or about my own reaction the next day. Which is, I suppose, an illustration of the old saying that anticipation is better than realization. Or that happiness is in the pursuit. Those were somewhat complex thoughts for an eleven-year-old, but I had a vague understanding of the principle even then. And I know that T did, too.

11
Exodus

A few weeks after Christmas, W.T. joined the C.C.C., the Civilian Conservation Corps, and was stationed at Tellico Plains in East Tennessee. Rebecca continued to live with Aunt Betty in Waverly leaving Mother, Margaret, Bettie, Bertha, Patsy and me on the farm. Suddenly, at twelve years of age, I was the man of the house.

I suppose everything would have gone along okay except for an extreme cold spell that caught us unaware. Our wood supply was ample to carry us through a normal winter, but when the temperature dropped near zero and continued to stay cold day after day, our woodpile dwindled rapidly. Finally the day came when there was no more firewood for the cook stove or the heater. Mother could do most anything except chop wood. So Margaret and I tried. The cold was so bitter that the ground crunched like glass and our ears and noses began to tingle and hurt within minutes after we went outside.

We went into the woods behind the smokehouse and tried to cut down a sapling two or three inches in diameter. But the ax bounced off the frozen wood harmlessly. Shivering and with our hands getting numb, the best we could do was chop up a few small branches and some rotting boards. These burned quickly without producing much heat. With night coming on, Mother was becoming desperate. Afraid to leave us or to send Margaret or me for help, she had us put on all the clothes we could wear and we all went outside and closed the door. She picked up Pat and led us to the path toward the Forrests'.

Other than the crunch of our footsteps there was hardly a sound in the cold, still woods and fields. We felt forlorn and fearful, and miserably cold. But there was no crying or whimpering from the little ones and hardly a word was spoken as we walked. Finally we trudged up the steps and knocked on the Forrests' door. Mr. Forrest and Miss Rose opened the door, stared at us in disbelief, then hurried us inside. Her strength exhausted, both physical and emotional, Mother broke down and cried.

The Forrests had a huge fireplace as well as a stove in their kitchen, where they spent most of their time when at home. It wasn't long before we were cozy and warm; enjoying the smell from a big pot of beans hanging in the fireplace and searching for funnies in the big barrel of newspapers a few feet from the fire. Before dark, they removed the tablecloth that had been thrown over the leftovers from the noon meal. Miss Rose added beans from the fireplace and bread from the "warming closet" over the stove for a bountiful meal. Then they "put us up" for the night. Pat, Bertha, Bettie and I slept in an upstairs bedroom on a thick featherbed soft as a cloud.

Of course Mother explained our plight, stressing that we would have been all right if the cold spell hadn't lasted so long. The next morning, after breakfast, she sent Margaret and me back home to feed Jersey and the chickens. That done, we looked around the kitchen to see if we could find something to eat ourselves. The peaches that Mother had "put up" in Mason jars were sitting on a shelf. The lids were about a half-inch above the tops of the jar, pushed up by the frozen peaches. That was in 1934 and I am writing this in 2001, but Margaret and I both still remember vividly standing in that cold kitchen eating the frozen peaches we pried from those jars.

We went back to the Forrests' to read more funny papers and eat another meal. Meanwhile, one of Mr. Forrest's sons and a son-in-law (Charlie Forrest and Revo Summers, I believe) had gone down to our house, chopped a huge pile of wood and built a fire in the heater. We walked back home that afternoon and settled back into our normal routine.

(In case I haven't done so before, I would like to mention that Mr. Forrest and Miss Rose were the parents of Uncle Tom Forrest, who was married to Aunt Betty.)

Sometime later Mother got a letter from Daddy saying that things were going well in Birmingham and that we should hire someone to move us there.

In preparation for moving, Mother decided we should gradually get rid of our chickens. Some way she learned that the "chicken man" would be at Warren's store on a particular day so she planned to take some of the chickens to sell at that time. Unfortunately, the creek was up. It had not washed out the foot log, but the surface of the water had reached the bottom of the log, making it unsafe to cross over. So Mother decided we would take the chickens by way of the swinging bridge.

In an exciting chicken chase we managed to catch six of the frantically clucking, scrambling hens. We tied their legs together and Mother took two in each hand while I took one in each. They struggled and flapped their wings until we held them upside down by their legs, at which time they became completely docile.

Because a lot of the floorboards had rotted away, walking the swinging bridge was a frightening experience at any time, but particularly so when the swollen creek flowed menacingly below and a chicken in each hand impeded the use of the cables that served as handrails. But we made it safely across the bridge and on to Warren's store.

I don't remember selling the cow, but I'm sure it was no problem because she gave as much as five gallons of milk a day. It may be that she was given to Dump Sykes as payment for moving us to Birmingham in his truck. The day came when he drove across the creek, helped us load our possessions, and we began the long, slow trip back to the Magic City.

12
The Magic City

Daddy always said that a man was a fool if he lived so far from his job that he couldn't walk home for lunch. So it was no surprise to find that the house he had found for us in Birmingham was near the creosote plant. It was three houses from the end of 52nd Street, almost directly behind the house on 51st Street where we had lived when I was six years old. It had five rooms and a bath, running water and electricity. It was a tremendous improvement over the Old Home Place. However, there was no water heater and heat was provided by small coal-burning fireplaces called "grates." We still had to heat water for baths on the wood-burning kitchen stove, and Mother still had to wash clothes in an iron pot in the backyard. We did not have a refrigerator or icebox.

There were only nine of us when we first moved into the house, but W.T. came home from the C.C.C. a few months later, so then there were ten. I believe T came home just before school started in 1935. He had completed only two grades of high school, so he enrolled at West End High School that fall, mainly, I think, for the purpose of playing football. Apparently he did not make the team, or perhaps Daddy and Freeman were not making enough to pay the bills, for T dropped out after a few weeks and went to work at the plant.

The C.C.C. had mailed home the major portion of T's

salary each month and now he, as well as Freeman, continued to place most of their earnings in the family coffers. The only specific incident I can remember where Freeman bought something unessential for his own use was when he ordered a cheap guitar from Sears & Roebuck. It may be that this occurred while we were still in Tennessee, for he used to get together as often as he could for "picking and singing," with Cecil Stanfill. But possibly only Cecil had a guitar then. Anyway, in Birmingham Freeman became quite an accomplished guitarist and began playing with a local band. For a while he got up at four o'clock in the morning and rode a streetcar downtown to play on an early morning radio program before he went to work. (At that time, all radio broadcasts were "live.") We never heard his broadcasts because we didn't have a radio.

However, one day a few months after T went to work he asked me to walk with him up to Vinesville, where Floyd lived. Floyd had told him that one of his neighbors had a radio for sale. It was an arch-topped table model, typical of that era. I don't remember the selling price, but I remember it seemed like a tremendous amount. And I remember my thrill when T bought it, and my excited anticipation as we carried it back home. I still never heard one of Freeman's broadcasts, perhaps because they were discontinued but more likely, because I didn't get up early enough.

Because Freeman and T were working during the day, and probably looking for female companions in the evenings, I generally saw them only at meals during this period. Fortunately, there were a number of boys about my age in the neighborhood.

William Crunk lived two houses south on 52nd Street. His sister, Beatrice, was about Bee's age and his sister, Jo Anne, about Pat's age. They often visited in our home and sometimes we visited in theirs. William became my best friend.

Glen and Tommy Lee lived directly behind us in the only house on a dusty, dead-end street that ran beside our house. They were fraternal twins, but not twins in appearance. Glen had blonde, reddish hair and a freckled complexion, while Tommy had black hair and smooth-toned skin. Their bare dirt yard made an excellent place for playing marbles, so William and I spent a lot of time there.

Kenneth Outlaw, Floyd's cousin, lived on the corner of 52nd Street and Terrace Q directly across the street from William. Kenneth was a year or two older than the rest of us and had an almost fanatic interest in aviation. He spent a great deal of time at Messer Field, the local airport, where he learned to fly by the time he was fifteen. But he was with us in most of our pursuits. Kenneth was the one who introduced us to "tennis." He made some wood paddles to use as racquets and drew lines in the dirt street in front of his house to represent a net and boundaries. Because there was very little traffic, some days we played for hours without interruption.

Anytime we were not involved with something else, we played an endless game of "Stick 'em Up, Bang." This was a mongrel combination of "Cowboy and Indians," "World War I" and "Mafia vs. F.B.I." Our guns were homemade, sawed out of wood. Some shot rubber bands, but the ammunition for most was simply a verbal "Bang." My favorite gun was a wooden pistol, which I called "Old Betsy." It's impossible to explain the rules of the game because they changed from day to day.

Another favorite game was "Kick the Can," which we usually played at night. Some of the girls joined us in that game, which possibly had something to do with our decision to play after dark. In this game someone kicks a can and while the one who was selected to be "It" retrieves the can, everyone else hides. Then "It" captures everyone he can find, but if anyone can kick the can again without being caught all the captives go free. An inept "It" could retain that title for the entire night. I know.

Sometimes we played under the corner streetlight, throwing rocks into the air to see the bats chase them almost to the ground. Or sometimes we would sit or lie under the streetlight and just talk. We pondered how the blind bats could follow the rocks, whether they ever crashed into the ground and whether they would bite. Or we discussed some other scientific subject of that sort. Sometimes, lying on our backs watching the sky, we waxed philosophic, during which a typical conversation might be:

"Who made the stars?"

"God."

"Then who made God?"

Like adults, we were better at asking questions than at providing answers.

Invariably as the night grew late, someone would say, "Whoever goes home first is a rotten egg."

This prolonged the meeting for an hour or so but then, as we all got sleepier, someone would suggest that we all leave at the same time. We were a little better than adults at practical compromise.

Several years ago I read an article in *Reader's Digest* titled, "Let Them Build Their Own Tents." The gist of it was the fact that there is more pleasure in building something than there is in possessing it. This reminded me of a magnificent tree house we built almost fifty years earlier in a huge oak tree across the street from Glen and

Tommy's house. This was a joint venture by Glen, Tommy, William, Kenneth and me. We scrounged boards and nails from every available source. We climbed the tree by nailing short boards on the trunk to serve as a ladder and began construction by nailing two-by-fours across a "V" formed by two large limbs some twenty feet from the ground. Then, without the benefit of OSHA* or any other government regulations, we built a substantial deck ten feet square. We added walls about four feet high, but never did get around to a roof. Our plan was to make a retractable rope ladder and knock the boards off the trunk of the tree. But God saw that it was not good and prevented us.

Building that tree house took several weeks, which were filled with the pleasure of anticipation and the satisfaction of incremental accomplishments. Once it was completed, however, our interest waned and we went back to marbles, tennis and Stick 'em Up Bang.

---

*Occupational Safety and Health Act.

13
Floyd, Oretta, and the 5-Minute War

It was a little more than a mile from our house on 52nd Street to Floyd's house on Vinesville Avenue. Almost every weekend some of us walked to his house or he walked to ours. He always had a pack of Lifesavers in his pocket, which is the first thing we thought about when we saw him, but he occasionally brought or sent a gift considerably more substantial than a candy mint. I remember once he sent us a case of twenty-four ten-ounce "soda pops" of various flavors. None of us was accustomed to carbonated beverages—I don't think I had drunk one since Daddy bought me a "soda pop" at the Clydeton General Store. They burned our noses and we drank them with difficulty, but each of us was determined to drink his share.

Floyd occasionally took me to a movie or bought me a shirt or a pair of pants. I didn't think about it at the time but, even though they didn't show it, I now suspect my siblings resented this partiality toward me. Particularly after Christmas in 1933. At that time I was sleeping in the living room (we had a bed in every room except the kitchen) and when I woke up Christmas morning I was elated and absolutely astonished to see a bicycle on the other side of the room. I knew immediately that it was from Floyd. It was a used bike, the inexpensive "single tire" type, with no fenders, and badly in need of paint. But it looked magnificent to me. In my wildest dreams I had not imagined getting a bike. Sixty years later, Floyd told me the bike cost him $1.50. Never has a dollar and a half bought more joy.

In the summer of 1934 Floyd took me with him on a vacation trip to McKinnon. We spent a week with his Aunt Mattie, where I got to ride a horse for the first time in my life, even riding her once over the steep bill behind Aunt Mattie's house and all the way to downtown McKinnon—two stores and a filling station. We visited Floyd's other relatives, including his Aunt Polly and cousin, Oretta. My infatuation with Oretta returned, even though she gave no impression of a similar feeling toward me. There was a new compelling element of physical magnetism, but she was the magnet and I was simply some random ferrous material. However, when I got back to Birmingham I wrote her a letter and she answered it.

I carried her letter in my shirt pocket for days and "carelessly" let it slip to my playmates that she and I were corresponding with each other. One day when we were all playing together, Kenneth started teasing me about Oretta, asking naughty questions about our relationship. As I responded indignantly, he snatched her letter from my pocket. I tried to retrieve the letter, but he evaded me easily, opening the letter as he ran, and then reading it out loud to the boys. He finally gave the letter back and I angrily went home.

I fussed and fumed to William about Kenneth's crudeness for days. Without too much enthusiasm, William allied himself with me and we decided to declare war. Since Kenneth probably could lick us both at the same time, we decided an ambush would be the best tactic. William had a tool shed in his back yard, sitting back about thirty feet from 52nd Street, and Kenneth walked by it almost every day. We decided this would be our fort. We stored an ample supply of rocks on the roof along with two garbage can lids to use as shields. Then one day when we saw Kenneth approaching we scrambled up onto the roof. We held our fire till we saw the whites of his eyes, then let fly a barrage of rocks. Our military tactics left a lot to be desired. We had not considered the fact that Kenneth would have an endless supply of rocks along the road, nor that he would be able to dodge in every direction while we were confined to a six-foot-square roof. Kenneth's return fire bombarded against our garbage can lids alarmingly. Then I failed to lower my shield enough to catch a low-flying rock, which hit my right shin like a sledge hammer. Crying out with pain, I scrambled back off the roof with William close behind me. We stayed hidden behind the shed, but we could hear Kenneth laugh as he walked away.

There was no apology from either side and no formal truce, but within a day or so peace prevailed. Two badly dented garbage can lids, my swollen shin and slight limp were the only remaining evidence of the great war.

14
West End

On our return to Birmingham, Bettie, Bee and I went to Central Park School, where Bettie and I had attended when we were in Birmingham before. Mr. Keenan was still the principal, but I don't know if Miss Burglar and Miss Stone were still teaching there or not. Nor can I remember becoming reacquainted with Billy Thomas, Lawrence George or David Hadden.

Margaret, Rebecca and for a while W.T. went to West End High School. To do this they had to walk a path through a field of high grass, bushes and trees at the end of 52nd Street. Then they crossed a railroad track and the creosote plant, a sprawling lot filled with cross ties and telephone poles in various stages of manufacture. After that was a wide but shallow stream, Valley Creek, which they crossed on stepping stones. After climbing a four-foot bank on the other side of the creek they walked another mile to the school. There was an elementary school adjoining the high school but, of course, Central Park School was much nearer to us. The school situation, and the fact that we had no place to keep a cow on 52nd Street, caused Daddy to look for another place to live. He found the ideal spot just on the other side of Valley Creek, on St. Charles Avenue.

The street name suggests an upscale neighborhood, but actually the house was in an area where the Depression had stopped the building of a subdivision in midstream. There were sidewalks and fireplugs over several blocks, but only a few houses—plenty of vacant lots where a cow could graze. We were not happy to leave our friends in Central Park, but we kept pointing out that we would still be in walking distance and there was an air of excitement about moving into a new house. New to us: It was quite apparently pre-used. It was a brick house, somewhat "nicer" than the one we vacated, but not larger. One of the most interesting features was a furnace, called an "Arcola" in a small room at the back of the house. This was supposed to furnish heat for the entire house. Unfortunately, it was out of order and we had to use small grates which had been installed for emergency use in individual rooms.

There was a separate garage, which became living quarters for our new cow, Daisy. And I became a cowboy again. Each morning my job was to stake out the cow in one of the vacant lots, then bring her in again for milking at the end of the day. Another chore, which usually fell to me, was to take about twenty-four pints of milk to the creosote plant at noon to sell to the workers for lunch. Mother packed the bottles in a flat box and it required considerable skill to balance this box while going down the bank and negotiating the stepping stones across the creek. It was particularly important not to jostle the milk when Mother used wax paper and rubber bands as stoppers. Less so when she used the regular bottle stoppers Floyd bought for her. The stoppers made the milk look as if it came from a dairy, and I felt quite professional delivering milk without the shabby-looking wax paper and rubber bands.

For a long time I went to Central Park to play with the old gang almost every day. Sometimes I would ride my bicycle, which quadrupled the distance because I had to go so far north to find a bridge across Valley Creek. When I rode my bike, sometimes Bee would go with me, riding on the crossbar, to visit Beatrice Crunk. Pat was too young for such journeys and Bettie was not interested because she had met a new friend, Helen Swaim, in West End. Helen was about Bettie's age, an absolutely beautiful little blonde, admired by all the boys and envied by all the girls. She was involved in my first "date." (See R-rated Chapter 15, *Revolting Hormones*.)

A divorced lady occupied the house next to us on St. Charles Avenue, almost a block away. As was customary in those days, she was sometimes referred to, in hushed tones, as a "grass widow." This status automatically gave her a certain mystique, which was magnified by the fact that her last name was Harlow—reminiscent of the movie star—and she had an expensive-looking automobile. Also she had a telephone.

Telephones were fairly commonplace, but Kenneth Outlaw was the only one of my acquaintances who had one. Once when I was visiting in Central Park, Kenneth suggested that the gang get together the next Saturday and go to the public swimming pool in Ensley. That Friday I wanted to confirm the time we were to meet, but I didn't want to walk all the way to Central Park to do so. I had never used a telephone, but decided I would ask Miss Harlow if I could call Kenneth. She graciously agreed, pointed to the phone and left the room. I knew Kenneth's number and had enough sense to lift the receiver and dial. But some strange lady answered and said she didn't know any Kenneth Outlaw. I figured his phone was out of order, or the telephone operator had made a mistake. So I hung up, thanked Miss Harlow, and left. It was several years before I tried to use a telephone again.

I got to Central Park in time to go with Kenneth, William, Glen and Tommy to the swimming pool. As we walked the four-mile distance I was torn with anticipation and dread. Floyd had taken me to a public pool before, so I knew how much fun it was, and I knew that all the boys, as well as I, would be wearing an undershirt with their trunks. (Boys and men were required to wear "tops.") But my sense of modesty and my self-consciousness about my skinny physique made me dread walking out of the dressing room into that crowd of boys and girls. It took all my will power to do so but once in the pool I enjoyed it immensely.

The pool was crowded with boys and girls of all ages, the older ones obviously more interested in flirting with each other than in swimming. I was far too timid to initiate such activity, and not nearly attractive enough to be the object of it. Mostly, the flirting consisted of "showing off" in various ways, but on one occasion Kenneth said, "If you want to see something, check that out," indicating a boy and girl standing by one of the ladder-like steps for climbing out of the pool. Only their heads were above water. At Kenneth's urging I swam underwater closer to them and was astonished to see the boy was feeling her in a very intimate way. I was more astonished to realize she was remaining submerged, willingly permitting it. I came to the surface looking purposely in the other direction, and hurriedly moved away.

We swam and cavorted in the pool most of the day without a break for lunch. None of us had money to buy lunch, anyway, but by the middle of the afternoon we were so hungry we decided to go home. As we walked, we talked about how hungry we were until some of us protested that it would be less painful if we didn't talk about food. But Kenneth tormented us by continuing to talk on and on about "soupy potatoes." I'd never been so hungry in my life. And when the others had reached home, I had another hard half-mile to go. Mother had an iron skillet on the stove with something in it for my lunch. I don't remember what it was. I ate it so fast I may not have noticed.

Having found the telephone so unreliable, I decided we needed a better way to communicate between West End and Central Park. I knew there was a direct line of sight between my house and our tree house in Central Park, so I came up with an idea. I built my own personal tree house in a chinaberry tree in our back yard. It was not magnificent like the one in Central Park—just one board nailed across two limbs about ten feet high. But it served the purpose. Then I found the Morse code in a book and laboriously wrote a copy for myself, and a copy for the yet-to-be designated telegrapher in Central Park. On my next trip, I explained my plan to Glen, Tommy, et al.: at a designated time each night we would man our Signal Stations and use flashlights to share the day's news by Morse code.

At the proper time that night I ascended to my tree house with flashlight and code in hand. I flashed a series of blinks in the direction of Signal Station #2 to let them know I was "on line," although that term would have made no sense in that era. After a short wait I was delighted to see a blinking light in the southern sky. My pencil was ready and I diligently wrote down the "dots" and "dashes." When they stopped, I flashed an "okay" and began decoding, printing the appropriate letters beneath the dots and dashes. I was elated when words began to appear: F-L-O-Y-D I-S C-O-M-I-N-G. Gleefully I scrambled down the tree and ran down the path toward the creek. Floyd was genuinely amazed when he discovered I knew he was on the way and showed him the message. I don't remember ever using the signal stations again but, for me, that one transmission ranks right up there with "What hath God wrought."

15
Revolting Hormones
(Parental notice: You probably shouldn't read this.)

September came. Margaret and Rebecca went back to West End High School and Bettie and I enrolled at Robert E. Lee Elementary. I remember very little about that school except that one incredibly stupid teacher, curious about the shape of my shoulders, asked if I had had polio. This intensified my self-consciousness about my physical appearance at a time when it was of tremendous importance because of an awakening interest in girls. Perhaps, however, it was another example of all things working together for good: if I had been physically attractive to girls, or had thought I was, I might have become an intolerable rogue. I made considerable progress in that direction, anyway.

After school started, I began to make fewer trips to Central Park and to spend more time with Cecil Kaiser, one of our nearest neighbors. He was a handsome, athletic young man; he was to the girls what Helen Swaim was to the boys, and I confess being envious of him, even though I liked him very much and we became close buddies.

There were a number of other boys who played with us, although I can't remember any of their names. Mostly we played baseball at the girls' reform school. Actually, I should say we played where the girls' reform school used to be. The rambling building was closed and vacant. We understood that they closed it because they didn't have enough bad girls to keep it open. If we had been a few years older that may not have happened.

The reform school was only a couple of blocks from our house, at the end of St. Charles Avenue. There was a high wire fence around the grounds, but the front gate was open and inside was a perfect spot for a baseball diamond. Usually we had enough for two teams of four or five each, and we were very fortunate in that there was never an adult in sight. The games were completely unorganized and great fun. I can't say that I was the first pick when we chose up sides, but I did enjoy playing until one day when I tried to catch a hard "grounder." God had other plans. The ball hit a pebble a few feet in front of me, bounced up at the speed of light and hit me square on the nose. I saw stars, planets, asteroids and blood. I continued to play baseball from time to time, but the fact that I never became an all-star player can be traced directly back to that incident.

Ever since I learned to read I had enjoyed reading. At that particular time I was enthralled with King Arthur stories. Cecil liked those stories also, and we did a lot of what I think is now called "role playing." We imagined that the old reform school building was a castle from which we rescued damsels in distress. And we fantasized, in a noble, knightly way, how those ladies would try to reward us for our heroism. Like Sir Galahad we would, of course, gallantly refuse their offers.

I was also reading a lot of pulp magazines, mainly *The Flying Aces,* which Kenneth Outlaw gave to me and which were stories of the aviators in World War I. Almost invariably, the ace would get shot down somewhere in France and become involved with some fetching mademoiselle. The story never explained exactly what he did with the girl but I imagined all sorts of things because the mademoiselle always begged for mercy. The aviator would start out by lighting a cigarette for her, or something like that, then the first thing you know she would be saying, "Merci, monsieur!"

I have given you this glimpse into the secret mind of a thirteen-year-old male so you will better understand that which follows. At about age thirteen, boys develop a dual thinking system. With one, they think about their normal activities such as studying, eating, playing or working, while with the other, simultaneously, they think about girls. Fortunately, this is a temporary condition, which ceases when they die.

My family had someway acquired a lawn mower. The reel-type lawn mowers of those days were designed incidentally to cut grass but mainly to give exercise to the operator. Cecil and I pushed that mower around the neighborhood and tried to convince our neighbors that we were men enough to be able to mow their lawns. We were successful only with the man who lived across the street from Miss Harlowe, a barber. He offered us ten cents. We cut his grass a number of times for that price, but we complained bitterly to each other that he got twenty-five cents to cut the hair on one head and we got only a dime to mow a lawn one thousand two hundred and fifty times that size. For comparative purposes, we assumed the average head was a foot square.

One other source of income was Miss Harlowe, who occasionally paid us a quarter to wash her car.

Apparently news of our wealth spread, because Helen Swaim and another girl, whose name I cannot remember, kept making hints that we should go on a "date." Eventually we set the time for one Saturday afternoon.

We met secretly and walked over to Central Park. We were not so gauche as to suggest they walk across the creek and the creosote plant, so we went the long way via the bridge. Cecil and I walked with dignity and carried on a calm and intelligent conversation, but we were compressing all sorts of urges and emotions inside. The girls beside us added tremendously to the pleasure we got watching the double feature, the newsreel, the chapter piece, the cartoon and the previews of coming attractions. I had sense enough to know you don't hold hands with a girl on the first date. But I thought about it. I even thought about putting my arm around her but, having a surplus of caution and a deficit of courage, I didn't follow through. There was an air of exhilaration as we walked home, and we agreed we had fun and that we should do it again. Fortunately for them, before we got around to doing so Daddy found a better-paying job in East Point, Georgia, and we left West End.

16
East Point

In 1937 Birmingham, The Magic City, and Atlanta, The Gateway to the South, were about the same size and jealous rivals. Somehow the employees at the American Creosote Plant in Birmingham discovered that the Southern Wood Preserving Company was hiring in East Point, Georgia, a suburb of Atlanta. For several families, their allegiance to Birmingham was inconsequential against the opportunity for better wages. Among those who migrated east were the Albrights, the Largins and the Stanfields.

Initially, only Daddy and W.T. made the move. They stayed at a boarding house for a few months, then found a house for sale directly across the street from the plant. Daddy did not believe in going into debt. I doubt that he had ever bought anything other than groceries on credit, and I suspect that W.T. did a lot of talking to convince him to buy that house. However, with Freeman, W.T. and Daddy all working, they decided we could afford to buy, and Daddy was delighted to find a place to live so close to his work. The price of the house was $1,200. Daddy made a down payment, financed the balance and, at forty-seven years of age, became a homeowner for the first time. The house was at 406 Chattahoochee Avenue. Ted Albright, who had worked with Daddy in Birmingham, had bought the house at 404, next door, and had moved in with his wife, Esserie, his two little boys and an automobile.

Since we had no telephone, I assume Daddy let us know by mail when he was ready for us to move to Atlanta. I don't remember how our furniture was moved, or how Freeman got there, but Mother, the girls and I rode the train. Mr. Albright and T met us at the Terminal Station and Mr. Albright drove Mother and the five girls to our new home in his car. T and I rode the trackless trolley. Unlike these days when innumerable buses traverse the streets of Atlanta with only two or three passengers in each, and empty rapid transit trains zip along their billion-dollar rails, the trolley was full and we had to stand for the six-mile trip.

From the trolley stop on Main Street, it was a quarter mile to our house. The house was an ugly brown on the outside and the woodwork on the inside was an ugly black. It had the typical five rooms and one bath, but a hallway in the center which was just wide enough for a bed. We had to crawl over the foot of the bed to get in it, but that is where T and I slept. We heated water on the wood cook stove and carried it to the bathtub in a pail. Mother still washed clothes in an iron pot in the back yard and, because we immediately bought a cow, she still had to milk. I still had the job of staking out the cow in our back yard or in the vacant land behind our neighbors next door. Though now homeowners, our living conditions remained about the same.

Our neighbors on our left were the Arnolds, who, with three generations plus in-laws living in their house, had about the same number as we. The Albrights were on our right and next to them the Blacks, who had three teen-age daughters and an older son. Mr. Largin, who had worked with Daddy in Birmingham, lived about a mile away, but later moved within two blocks. One of his two sons, Marvin, was my age and became a close friend. Leon McGouirk, whose family was related to the Arnolds by marriage, lived a half-mile down the road but almost every day rode his bike up to my house—possibly attracted by my five sisters. He and I became constant companions. There were other families with children in our neighborhood, so we had an abundance of friends, most in economic circumstances not much better than ours.

As our financial condition gradually improved, Mother insisted on painting the house white inside and out. This brightened the whole house, including our cramped bedroom. Daddy had coils installed in the firebox so that water was heated anytime there was a fire in the stove. The heated water was stored in a standard water tank with pipes going to the bathroom and kitchen sink.

For the first time that I could remember, Daddy sometimes joined us in strictly recreational activities. The family income covered daily expenses and we had reasonably comfortable living conditions. We were directly across the street from Daddy's work and the plant had a shower room where he could bathe and change clothes before coming home. Finally he had a little time to relax. Together, we and the Arnolds built a horseshoe court between our houses and strung up electric lights so we could play at night. The Albrights and some of the other neighbors joined in and we would sometimes have fifteen or twenty people under the lights on a pleasant summer night. Daddy loved the game, and was quite skilled at pitching "ringers". Mother didn't play, but she joined the spectators regularly. Having congenial neighbors, and having less worry about money, she was more relaxed than she had been in years.

At night it was mostly the adults who pitched horseshoes, but Leon McGouirk and I played many hours during the day. After we had started making a little money mowing lawns, we began to bet as to who would win. On one occasion I lost my entire fortune of $1.50.

We went all over East Point mowing lawns, with the same back-breaking mower that Cecil Kaiser and I had used in West End. But being a little older, Leon and I got more jobs and charged enough to be able to go to a movie about once a week and drink at least one "Spinning Wheel" malted milk at the Miss Georgia ice cream store.

Most Sundays I spent with W.T., and the thing we did most was walk. Many times we walked to the airport, about two miles, to watch the planes come and go. This was such a popular pastime that there was an observation platform on the terminal building for the public. We walked to Adams Park, where the attraction was a public swimming pool well stocked with pretty young girls. And we walked to the Chattahoochee River, about twelve miles, looked at the river and walked back home. The main pleasure in that trip was stopping at a little wayside store just before the river to buy a bag of peanuts and a Seven-Up. Sometimes Daddy or other members of the family went with us to the airport or to Adams Park, but no one else felt it was worth it to walk twenty-four miles, total, for a bag of peanuts and a soft drink.

The first summer in East Point was a generally happy time and went very quickly. The one sorrowful time for me was when I learned that my Birmingham friend, Tommy Lee, had been killed. He and his twin brother, Glen, were riding a bicycle and had run in front of a car on Bessemer Boulevard. Although I had gone to the funeral of Uncle Pierce Hooper, Aunt Mamie's husband, when I was ten, I really hadn't known him. So this was my first personal encounter with the reality of death. It was a sobering experience.

17
School, Magic, Bike, and Boat

Before school started in 1937 I was in something of a quandary. The school system in Birmingham required eight years of elementary school before four years of high school. The Fulton County, Georgia, system required only seven years before high school. I had been double promoted that is, skipped one semester, in Birmingham but still needed one semester of elementary school before being eligible for high school in East Point. So the question was whether I had a half a year too many or a half a year too few. Rather than confuse the authorities, I simply went to Russell High School as if that's where I belonged. They asked me no questions and I told them no lies.

My enrollment counselor was Miss Starr, who lived only a block from us toward Main Street on Chattahoochee Avenue. She decided I should take the Scientific Course plus R.O.T.C.* I didn't even know they had different "courses." If I had, I probably would have selected the Classical Course—languages, literature, etc. and no R.O.T.C. But the military program proved to be of very practical value in that, beginning the second year, the school furnished a uniform. This was worn to school every day except Friday and, besides the economic bene-

*Reserve Officers' Training Corps.

fit, avoided embarrassing conspicuousness for those like me who could not afford "nice" clothes.

The girls did not have this benefit but, thanks to Mother's sewing ability and good taste, they dressed reasonably well. However, Rebecca did not attend her own graduation ceremony in 1938 because she couldn't afford a formal gown. Margaret did have a dress and participated in the ceremony when she graduated the next year. Rebecca went with her to a photographer and they shared the same dress for graduation pictures. Being in elementary school and having the benefit of hand-me-downs, clothes were of less concern to the younger girls. Bettie and Bee attended Central Park Elementary School. Pat began in the first grade at Colonial Hills, and many mornings Mother encouraged her to go with a few stripes from a hickory switch. Frequently I took her to or from school on my bike.

I was a good student, but not particularly zealous. I always listened attentively to the teacher and was able to maintain good grades with a minimum of study outside the classroom. Quite frequently I missed a day of school to stay home and practice juggling or magic tricks. I had no instructions of any sort on juggling and I used ping pong balls for practice. This made it many times more difficult to learn than it would have been if I had used heavier balls, and I never became very proficient. However, I could juggle up to four balls reasonably well. I had no tutor for magic and had never seen a magician perform except on two brief occasions. One was on the street in Birmingham when I was seven years old, and one was in school when I was in the fifth grade. At that time, Paul Bolen, a one-legged veteran from World War I, gave a magic show at Central Park School. I did not have the nickel needed to attend the show, but he came around to the classroom to give a free preview, and I was absolutely fascinated when he made coins and balls disappear "right before our eyes."

In *Popular Mechanics* magazine I saw an advertisement for a book on coin magic by T. Nelson Downs, King of Koins. The price was ten cents; postage was three cents, so it was in my financial range. I missed a few more days of school because of that book, but I became quite proficient doing sleight-of-hand magic with coins. Floyd, who had become acquainted with magician Paul Bolen in Birmingham, sent me "Color-changing Knife" and a set of "Multiplying Balls," which put me well on my way toward becoming the Greatest Magician in the world living in East Point.

Being able to "amaze" my friends helped me to overcome feelings of inferiority that had plagued me ever since I could remember. This was not pathological; I recognized that I was equal or even superior to my friends and classmates in some ways, but I was painfully aware of my inadequate physical appearance, obvious poverty, and lack of social skills. When I pushed these concerns into my subconscious it seemed that some little incident would reawaken them. On one occasion in my sophomore year one of my classmates a "macho" football player, derisively asked, "What happened to your chest?"

My first impulse was to say, "What happened to your brain," but instead I said, "It's congenital." Then added, "That means I was born this way."

The subtle insult went completely over his head, but his comment bothered me for weeks. So much so that I went to a pharmacy downtown where I had seen a window advertisement for shoulder braces. They had a physical therapist in an upstairs office, and he was a very understanding man. He gave me some suggestions to improve my posture, and taught me to walk putting one foot directly in front of the other instead of at a "slew-footed" angle. He also sold me a brace, which apparently was originally designed for use in a medieval torture chamber. I wore it for a while, but it cut into my shoulder painfully, particularly when I rode my bicycle, and restricted the use of my arms. Also, it became apparent that it would do nothing to correct the bone structure which was my problem.

Apparently I had worn out my $1.50 bicycle because we did not move it from Birmingham to East Point. But a few months after we moved, Floyd left Pizitz Department Store, and went to work for Wimberly Thomas Hardware Company. This was a wholesale distributor and they handled bicycles. Even though he could get it wholesale, and probably got an employee discount as well, I could hardly believe it when Floyd shipped me a brand new, bright and shiny, "double tired" bike.

After getting that new bike, instead of walking to the Chattahoochee River, T and I rode—at least down hills. He pedaled and I rode sitting sideways on the crossbar. This decreased our travel time to about an hour and a half each way.

T decided that we should build a boat. He didn't claim that God told him to do this, and the specifications came from *Popular Mechanics* rather than a Divine decree, but he had something of the same determination that Noah had in regard to the ark. And some of the same faith: We were twelve miles from the river, had no automobile and sure couldn't transport that boat on a bike. Our neighbors weren't as derisive as Noah's, but they did ask some skeptical questions when the boat began to take shape on the sawhorses in our back yard. It turned out amazingly well for someone with no previous experience. T kept the side boards wet and rigged a method of bending them a little each day until they came to a point at the bow and curved slightly inward at the stern. The bow sloped up gracefully so it was an attractive as well as functional boat. Mr. Albright volunteered to take it to the river atop his car and after it became water-soaked it didn't leak a drop. We left it tied near the Fairburn Road bridge, and several times T and I made bicycle trips for an hour or so of floating on the river. One time Mr. Albright drove us with Mother and Daddy and two or three of the girls for a picnic and a "cruise."

Then we decided the boat would be less likely to be stolen if we moved it to a spot adjacent to a farm owned by Andy McGouirk, Leon's uncle, about a mile upstream. Freeman, W.T., Howard McGouirk and I went out one hot summer Sunday to make the move. Staying close to the shore, we laboriously paddled and pulled. Once a snake dropped into the boat from an overhanging branch. Tired, mosquito-bitten and wet with sweat, we finally tied the boat at our destination, then walked across an endless stretch of plowed fields to the farmhouse, hungry as bears. Annie McGouirk served us a supper of boiled potatoes, cornbread and coffee.

The boat was stolen sometime within the next few days.

18

Selling Wood, Football, Boxing, and Girls

In the winter, when there was no grass to cut, Leon and I worked for Hight (last name unknown). Hight had a sawmill in the vacant lot on the other side of the Arnolds', consisting of an old auto mounted on blocks with a drive belt around a rear wheel leading to a large circular saw. The creosote plant sold or gave him all the cull telephone poles and all the waste from their manufacture. During the week, Hight and some older boys, including Kenneth Arnold, sawed and split this material into stove wood and loaded it onto two stake-body trucks.

Before dawn on Saturday mornings a half dozen of us younger boys clambered atop the loads of wood and began delivering to black neighborhoods around Atlanta. An eighty-year-old black man, George Churn, walked in front of the slowly moving trucks selling wood to the residents, who came out to the street to place their orders when they heard us coming. We loaded the wood into square baskets. The price was ten cents for one basket, fifteen cents for two baskets, and twenty-five cents for three. George referred to these quantities as "ten pounds," "fifteen pounds," etc. and yelled out the orders, "Fifteen pounds ovah thar! Twenty-five pounds ovah hyar! Fifty pounds thar."

One boy stayed on the truck to reload empty baskets

while the rest of us scurried back and forth into the shanties and apartments delivering the wood. At midday we stopped at a little neighborhood grocery and bought a Moon Pie and a Big Orange for lunch. That consumed ten cents out of a dollar we were paid for the day. When a truck was emptied it was sent back for another load, so it was always well after dark before we were back home.

My new bicycle increased the hunting range for Leon and me in our endless quest for girls. We added the Oakland City swimming pool to our list of viewing areas, and spent many summer hours looking at the girls there through the high wire fence that surrounded the pool. Sometimes we rode to Kress's in downtown Atlanta, ostensibly to visit Rebecca, who was working there part time, but actually to ogle the other girls. In those days, managers consciously hired attractive girls, so there really were a lot of "million-dollar babies in the five-and-ten-cent store." We walked around the store and when a clerk asked, "May I help you?" we grinned wickedly (we thought) and said, "We're just looking."

We pedaled occasionally all the way to Fairburn, almost twenty miles south, where we actually met two girls, Anne Duke and one whose name I can't remember. They borrowed bikes and went riding with us. It was good physical exercise, and an exercise in futility for our pubescent fantasies.

We played football with the local boys. Mostly in a vacant lot around the corner on Maple Street. I was too light to be much of a lineman and not skilled enough to do very well throwing and catching passes. But I really enjoyed football. At least until the day when Loretta Starr (no relation to the teacher) and several other girls were watching us play and I intercepted a pass. I was well on my way to a touchdown with not another player within ten feet.

My brain, thinking about Loretta Starr, forgot to direct my right foot, which hooked itself around my left foot for a spectacular one-man tackle.

Somebody in the neighborhood came into the possession of a set of boxing gloves, and we sometimes had amateur bouts in my back yard. Those were the days of Max Schmeling and Joe Louis. When a boxing match was on, everybody huddled around the radio. The Golden Gloves Tournaments were in their heyday and we all knew that the Marquis of Queensberry rules did not permit hitting below the belt. Occasionally I sparred gently with Leon or one of the other boys we normally played with, but none of us had boxing experience and we feinted more than we hit. One day a slightly older boy, whose name I have willfully forgotten, talked me into donning the gloves with him. Not that it made any difference in the outcome, but he had considerable experience boxing at the YMCA. I blocked his first blow with my nose—the same nose that had stopped a bouncing baseball about a year earlier. That ended my boxing career, accelerated the tendency of my nose to droop and negatively affected my facial beauty.

During his second year in high school, Leon decided to drop out and go to work with his father at Southern Saw Works. He found sharpening saws to be more interesting than sharpening his mind, and more lucrative. Shortly after going to work he bought a 1932 Chevrolet. This increased our opportunities in girl-hunting exponentially. Or perhaps I should say *his* opportunities. I can remember only two successful safaris in which I was involved. One of these was driving Anne Duke and that girl whose name I can't remember to the Band Day festivities at North Fulton High School. It was extremely cold and, fortunately, the 1932 Chevrolet did not have a heater. Helpfully, Anne and I generated enough heat in the back seat to warm the whole car. The other occasion was when we attended the Southeastern World's Fair at Lakewood in September, 1941. Ever vigilant to help others, Leon and I discovered that Hazel and Jessie Watts were at the fair without transportation home. We offered our services, which they happily accepted. We discovered there is no chaperone more efficient than a sister. Nevertheless, Hazel and Jessie remained our friends through the war years, which were soon to follow.

19
Vacations and Girls

Rebecca and Margaret were at the "dating" age, and they were very self-conscious about our plain, crowded home and the fact that we lived in an area where the pungent smell of creosote filled the air. About 1939 the name of our street was changed from Chattahoochee Avenue to Connally Drive. I remember Rebecca telling, with laughter but a touch of bitterness, how a boy had commented when she gave him her address, "Connally Drive! That sounds like a ritzy section."

Our austere conditions were much harder on Margaret and Rebecca than the boys and the younger girls. I was so busy with my own pursuits—figurative and literal—that I didn't pay too much attention to how Margaret and Rebecca occupied their time. I know they sometimes went places with the older McGouirk boys, Leon's cousins and their friends. And many nights a bunch of boys and girls gathered on our front porch to play Canasta. Another social function was "tying tags." The father of their friend, Agnes Archer, had a contract with a company to attach strings to cardboard price tags for use in tying the tags to merchandise. Agnes brought boxes of tags to our house and a gang of boys and girls would sit around laughing and talking while tying tags for some fabulous fee like one cent per ten tags.

Pat, Bee and Bettie had many young friends in the

neighborhood and were busy with them constantly. His work and his music consumed Freeman's time, and W.T. always had some project going in addition to his work. I was the most fortunate in that I got to visit Floyd in Birmingham a couple of times and he took me to McKinnon for a vacation in 1938. Oretta and I were fifteen years old and teen-age chemistry was definitely at work. She was the catalyst but not an affected ingredient.

In 1939 T took me on a vacation with him. We rode a Greyhound bus to Waverly and walked from the station to Uncle Will Fry's place on Little Richland Creek. Uncle Will was Mother's only brother, an easy-going, laconic man, a sort of "character," who wore overalls all the time and walked or hitch-hiked wherever he went. He was a "natural born" mechanic, known all over the county, and made a modest living by repairing farm implements, boat motors and lawn mowers when he wasn't busy hunting or fishing. His wife, Lydia (Aunt Liddy), was a plain country woman who said exactly what she thought, often in somewhat salty language. She was a great cook and spent most of her time cooking on a big wood-burning stove for visiting relatives and friends. Jean and Jo McNeil, two of Aunt Liddy's nieces, were visiting while T and I were there. They were identical twins, about a year younger than I and cute as buttons. We had a tremendous vacation and, of course, I fell in love with the twins. Uncle Will, who loved baseball, had a ball and gloves, so we played catch, I showed them magic tricks, and we played in the creek. My greatest thrill was wading the creek with Jo sitting on my shoulders.

The following summer, T and I decided we would visit Uncle Will and Aunt Liddy again. This time we decided to make it a real adventure by riding bicycles instead of taking the bus. T borrowed Leon McGouirk's bike and early one August morning, we set out. I was amazed that Mother permitted us to go. I think she didn't realize what a daunting task it would be to pedal 250 miles. Neither did we. This was before multiple-speed bikes with gear shifts had been invented, so we very shortly found ourselves pushing the bikes up hills.

We wore short-sleeve shirts; we had no hats or caps and the August sun bore down with a vengeance. I sunburned easily and could feel my face burning and see my arms turning red. We had not thought to bring water bottles and there were long stretches along old Highway 41 where there were no stores or service stations where water would be available. Once we drank with some misgiving from a small stream near the highway, not knowing what sort of impurities it might contain. By the middle of the afternoon we were still several miles from Cartersville, and near the point of exhaustion. A tire on T's bike suddenly went flat and, almost simultaneously, the chain broke on mine. Proving once more that all things work together for good.

We pushed the crippled bikes until we reached a little country store with colorful chenille bedspreads displayed on clotheslines. The owner was very courteous and agreed to store our bikes until we returned for them. We started walking north but almost immediately a farmer driving a truck gave us a ride to Cartersville. Fortunately, T had enough money to buy round trip tickets to Waverly on the Greyhound bus. We had to wait several hours in the bus station, and I amused myself practicing sleight-of-hand. Once I noticed a teen-age boy watching me and nonchalantly "vanished" a half-dollar. His eyes widened in surprise and I yawned with feigned boredom.

It was morning before we reached Waverly and walked the five miles out Highway 13 to Uncle Will's house. He was splitting stove wood when we walked up. He looked us over with studied indifference and murmured to me, "What you doing here, you long hungry thing?"

Later Uncle Will got me to one side and, obviously curious about our sunburned, disheveled appearance, said, "John C., did y'all hop a freight train up here?"

As luck would have it, they were expecting Jean and Jo to arrive for a visit the next day. Being still tired out, we slept late the following morning and were pleasantly awakened by the sound of Jean and Jo talking and laughing in the kitchen. We had a great time—swimming, talking, and eating. Two highlights I remember: one was when we went to the little store up the road from Uncle Will's place and he got me to show a trick to a group of farmers gathered around the cracker barrel. I put a half dollar in a Coke bottle, then shook it out and passed it around for their inspection. To that unsophisticated audience, it was an absolute miracle.

I enjoyed the other highlight even more. Jo and I happened to be in the kitchen alone and she was eating a slice of cantaloupe. She remarked about how good it was. I said, "Let me taste it!" and kissed her square on the lips. She was completely startled and, truthfully, I was, too. I felt my face flushing at my impulsive boldness but she laughed without reprimand and seemed pleased.

The week ended and we regretfully caught the Greyhound back to Cartersville. We bought the necessary equipment to fix the flat and repair the chain, then hitchhiked out to the chenille bedspread place. It wasn't so horribly hot as it had been the week before, so we made it back to East Point in good shape.

20

The Texas Connection

After living in Trinity a few years, Granddaddy Fry with his unmarried daughters moved to Alvin, Texas, where he opened a harness repair shop. We know that Mother lived in Alvin at least a year but we do not know how she came to be living in Trinity again when she and Daddy married. There is no one living today who knows the details of movements of the Fry family members prior to 1940. But in 1940 Granddad was operating the Fry Hotel in downtown Alvin and, still living there with their families were Aunt Nancy Latham, Aunt Lois Jackson, Aunt Erma McKeel (widowed) and Aunt Bertha Bovee. Aunt Kate Outlaw was in Birmingham and Mother was in East Point. Uncle Will Fry still lived near Trinity.

Grandfather Fry died in 1940. Mother and Aunt Kate took the two-day trip to Alvin by Greyhound bus for the funeral. I remember it well, because Mother continued to grieve for days after she got back home. None of us had seen Granddad Fry for many years (I really couldn't remember him at all) so our grief was only in sympathy for Mother and Aunt Kate. After their visit to Alvin, Aunt Bert and her husband, who she always called "Mr. Bovee," drove to East Point to visit us. They had no children, but they brought along Aunt Lois and her children, "Babe," "Sugar," Opal and "Boy." I don't remember what kind of car Mr. Bovee had, but it must have been a monster. When they returned to Texas they took Margaret and Rebecca, making a total of nine people in that car. Rebecca returned home by Greyhound after a week or so, but Margaret took a job working as a carhop at a drive-in restaurant. She stayed two or three months. An undated letter from her to Mother, written on lined tablet paper reads as follows:

Dear Mother,
Guess what? I got a job. I started last night. It's at Hellman's Café. He pays $1.00 on the inside and 50 cents on the outside. I worked inside from 4 to 9 and then on outside. I made $1.40 in tips from 9 to 12. Pretty good, huh? I think he is going to let me work on outside most of the time. Hope so because they don't ever tip you on the inside. We get 2 meals. I hope he lets me work from 4 to 12 all of the time because you make a lot more.

I will have to get a uniform. They cost $16 new but I might buy the girl's that is quitting. (She is getting married.) She wants $12 for it but I don't think it's worth it and besides I don't think it will fit. They have real satin skirts pleated and white satin blouses with a lot of stuff on it military style. Hers is worn almost through at pockets. I haven't got a thing to work in until I get a dress. Aunt Emma bought me a dress & made it & I wore it last night. My blue dress is worn out. Ladell & I are going to get a room together. We are staying together now in a man's room that is in New York. He is coming back soon so we will have to get out. Aunt Erma is going to fix us up a room. Ladell pays her $2.50 per week.

Has daddy got a job yet? What does W.T. do and is Freeman still teaching?

Is Tom Jr.* still in B'ham?

I don't know what to do about that uniform. I hate to pay that much for a worn out uniform but I hate to pay $16 for a new one.

Mary McKeel is supposed to come back next week. Hope she does.

Aunt Bert is still out in the country. Uncle Bovee says he can't breathe in the big city of Alvin. He wants to stay out in the wide open spaces. So I guess they will stay.

Did that storm do much damage around Atlanta? Boy the wind really did blow here.

Margaret

P.S. Sun. Worked last night on inside. Made 50 cents in tips. That's good for inside. He said he wanted to break me in on inside. Worked from 9 to 11 on outside. Made $1.35 tips Sun. nite.

When Margaret came home, Babe (whose real name is "Ladell") came with her and stayed a couple of weeks. She was a very pretty girl with a bubbling personality and I had to continually remind myself that she was my first cousin.

*Tom Latham, Aunt Nancy's son.

21
Increasing Income

After Margaret returned from Texas she went to work for Southern Bell Telephone Company, where Rebecca had worked since shortly after she graduated from high school. They worked as telephone operators and most of the time they worked "split shifts." This system was designed to get the very most from an employee for the very least amount of pay. They were scheduled to work four hours during the busy morning hours, go home four hours during the less busy time, then return for the evening rush. I believe they were paid fifteen cents for trolley fare, but nothing for the hour and a half travel time.

With the older children supporting themselves and also contributing to family needs, we were no longer struggling simply to buy food and shelter. We still did not have gas heat, a refrigerator or a car, but we had plenty of wood and coal, an icebox and, because Margaret and Rebecca were working for Southern Bell, a telephone. We went to the movies frequently, and Daddy subscribed to the newspaper. Bee was taking tap dancing lessons, something of a status symbol in those Shirley Temple days. I remember Daddy building a set of stage steps, weighing approximately two tons, for one of her "recitals."

Mother's favorite pastime was going to the movies, which she had rarely done before. The Fairfax Theater, about a mile from our house, had a "prize night" every Wednesday, with each ticket they gave an envelope containing anything from one cent to five dollars. So many Wednesday nights Mother and I (or one of the girls) walked to the "show." We saw a lot of good movies and a lot of bad ones, and once got a quarter in a prize envelope.

In 1939 when the *Gone With the Wind* premiere was held in Atlanta, Mother rode the trolley downtown with Pat, Bee, Bettie and two or three of the Arnold children. They left hours ahead of time to get a good spot in front of the Paramount Theater to see the arrival of the stars. But the long wait was wasted when they were pushed back from the curbside by more aggressive spectators. A kind gentleman hoisted Pat to his shoulders, so she and Mother, who was five-feet-eleven, got a few glimpses, but the other girls saw only the back of the other spectators. A few hours earlier my high school R.O.T.C. unit had served as honor guard at the airport as Clark Gable, Vivien Leigh and company walked from their plane to the terminal. When the young Olivia DeHavilland passed by, hardly an arm's length away, our eyes met and she smiled. I think it was a case of love at first sight, but she could do nothing about it because they were waiting for her at the Paramount.

Generally, everything was going quite well for us all. Apparently, however, all was not sweetness and light at the creosote plant. Around 1940 the workers went on strike. I don't know the reasons, but the fact that Daddy participated in the picket line leads me to believe the reasons were ample. Daddy was not a "union man" in the socialistic sense. He had been a supporter of free enterprise, and a Republican, all his life. When I was five years old I went with him to the Clydeton General Store to vote. Someone asked him who he voted for and one of my earliest memories is hearing his reply, "I voted for Herbert Hoover."

He thought Franklin Roosevelt was ruining the country by taking money from those who earned it and giving it to those who didn't. He was dead set against "redistribution of the wealth" even though most of his life he would have been on the receiving end. So when he joined in walking the picket line I know the grievances were real. The strike was settled and Daddy continued to work for Southern Wood. However, Margaret's letter to Mother quoted above indicates that he was out of a job sometime in 1940. Apparently he was just laid off because of a lack of work, for later he went to work for Southern Wood in Macon and Freeman went to work there also. They lived in a boarding house in Macon, but came back to Atlanta by Greyhound bus most every weekend.

Earlier Mother had talked Daddy into "boxing in" one end of the back porch to make an extra room. That and the fact that Daddy and Freeman were gone during the week, made the house somewhat less crowded than it had been. Mrs. Arnold was aware of this and she asked Mother if she would rent a bedroom to her aged parents. Throughout our years of deprivation Mother was constantly looking for ways to supplement our income, so she readily agreed.

Margaret and Rebecca, particularly Rebecca, had a fit. But the agreement was made and Mr. and Mrs. Russell-Howland moved into the front bedroom. They were a delightful old couple, probably in their nineties, and kept quietly to themselves. However, they did have to be worked into the schedule for our one bathroom and we were constantly aware of their presence. This development was a definite regression in our slow progress toward a more pleasant and more comfortable home. This was helped to some extent when W.T. also went to work at Southern Wood in Macon and, in any event, the Russell-Howlands stayed with us only a few months.

22
Freeman, Me, and W.T.

If they had been characters in the Bible parable, Freeman would have been the eldest son and W.T. the prodigal. That's extreme hyperbole, because they only remotely resembled those characters, but the comparison gives a good idea as to the differences in their personalities. Freeman was serious minded and deliberate, he seldom did anything impulsively and never without considering how it would affect the family. T was inclined to do things on the spur of the moment without too much thought as to the consequences. I remember one occasion the second time we were in Birmingham when T, then about sixteen, decided to visit Uncle Will in Tennessee. I don't know the details, but apparently he left, hitchhiking, against Mother's wishes. I remember Mother crying and the rest of us worrying until he was safely back home.

Because I cannot remember Freeman going from Birmingham to East Point with Daddy and T or riding with us on the train, I think that he remained temporarily on his job in Birmingham. However, it was not long before he joined us in East Point and went to work at Warren Refrigeration Company in Atlanta. Also, he immediately became involved with other guitar players. He took lessons from King Komokoloea, who had a popular music studio in Atlanta. Freeman was such an excellent student that His Majesty hired him part time to teach. Apparently

Freeman was not a very good teacher, however, for when he tried to teach me to play he failed miserably.

Freeman did a lot of things for me when I was a little boy, like building a truck wagon, a sled for a mud slide and shelves for my play store. In East Point, though, because he was most always at work or associating with his musical friends, I was not with him a great deal. I do remember once he, T and I went to the fair together at Lakewood Park. We had no extra money to spend, so walked around, just looking. At one exhibit, T started talking to a young girl, who appeared to be alone. Her boyfriend appeared unexpectedly and began to curse at T for flirting with his girl. T said, "Sorry, fellow, I was just being friendly."

But the guy, apparently showing off for his girl, and being considerably bigger than T, continued cursing and raised his fists threateningly. Freeman, who was six-feet-four, pushed T aside, moved forward aggressively and said, "Okay, buddy, you want to fight, bring it on!"

The boyfriend decided to take his girl to another exhibit.

Freeman was the first of the children to go to work and, initially I think he simply turned most of his income over to Daddy or Mother. T helped pay the bills, of course, but was more inclined to buy things on his own. He bought our first radio when we were still in Birmingham and, in East Point he bought, among other things, our first floor lamp, a set of encyclopedias and a typewriter. T never learned to type, but Rebecca, Margaret and I benefited from that typewriter. One of the few accomplishments that I feel comfortable bragging about is learning to type—with all fingers and no lessons—on T's typewriter.

In 1940 T bought a bulk lot of radio parts and tools

from Earl Godwin, who was liquidating his ham radio shop and going into the Marines. All T knew about a radio was how to turn it on and tune a station, but he was fascinated with the idea of building radios and owning all those tools. I shared this fascination. Somehow we convinced Mother to permit us to take over a large walk-in closet as a workshop. We built a work bench and spent hours sorting out the screws, nuts, bolts, tubes, condensers, resistors, etc. and learning how to build a radio. We actually completed one set on which we could listen to one local station. It had earphones instead of a speaker, and I remember listening to *The Jack Benny Program,* while lying in bed.

T bought one thing that we all got mad at him about. When he, Freeman and Daddy were working in Macon, Daddy and T rode the Greyhound bus home almost every weekend. Freeman also came sometimes, but to save bus fare, and because he was so involved with his job and music in Macon he came less often. As T was riding the Greyhound bus, I think he noticed macho guys passing by on motorcycles with good-looking girls wrapped around them in a most provocative way. So one day T rode up to 406 Connally Drive on a monstrous Harley-Davidson. It was exciting as a circus, and family and neighbors clustered around admiring his new toy.

But after the excitement died down, we started thinking about the fact that he could have bought an automobile for less than he paid for the motorcycle and then Daddy and Freeman could have ridden with him. We didn't hesitate to let him know what we thought, and he didn't hesitate to let us know it was his business to decide how he wanted to spend his own money. He was right, but we were mad at him anyway. He had never ridden a motorcycle before buying this one, so he was obviously unsure of himself as he rode. He didn't offer to let anyone ride with him until the next time he came up from Macon. But then I climbed up behind him and we rode down to the airport.

A couple of blocks from the airport as we made a right turn we hit some gravel in the road and the motorcycle slid out from under us. T apparently turned the throttle as we fell and the bike took off, spinning round and round in the street. T chased it down and got it back under control. Except for scratches on my right leg, neither of us was hurt. We got back on the bike and he very carefully drove home. Someway he got it up the steps and parked it on the front porch. I don't remember how long it stayed there, but long enough that we started calling it the "white elephant." The East Point Police department considered buying it, but decided against it. However one of the officers had a girlfriend who was a bike rider and she eventually bought it.

I still think T should have bought a car but, on reflection, I understand why he bought a motorcycle instead. He was twenty-four years old and had been helping support the family since he was sixteen. He had never owned a car, or even driven one, and probably felt he was being left out of the adventure and excitement of youth. The motorcycle looked like a quick way in. Two things caused him to change his mind: one was recognizing the danger involved, and the other was getting a draft notice from FDR.

23
Last Year at Russell

My best friend at Russell was Alan Rickerson. He was handsome, well built, and very intelligent. We were in some classes together and hung around together on the campus during free time and at lunch. We had many "intellectual" discussions and shared vague fantasies about becoming writers. We studied Journalism, and shared the job of Sports Editor on the school newspaper. Southern Wood Preserving Company sponsored a contest each year in which they gave $15 prizes to the two Russell High Seniors who wrote the best essays on "Patriotism." In 1941 Alan and I won those prizes. When the Journalism Class sponsored a variety show for the school, Alan and I did a memory and mind reading act, using methods I had learned in magic. Paul West, the principal of the school, who later became Superintendent of Education, was widely known for his prodigious memory (anecdotes abound as to how he would recognize a student by name many years after graduation). He complimented me on the memory portion of our act, obviously impressed.

In 1941 the student population at Russell High was approximately 600. Boys and girls attended classes together, but the boys were required to enter at one entrance and the girls at another. In the cafeteria, boys sat on one side and girls on the other. The campus was divided into two sections, one for girls and one for boys.

Alan and I brought our lunches and ate outside, along with perhaps half the student body. Eating our lunch each day and looking longingly toward the Promised Land, we decided this segregation was unconstitutional—cruel and unusual punishment.

After discussing this over a period of weeks we decided to petition for the redress of our grievances. We typed out several copies of a document, which rivaled the Declaration of Independence in eloquence, and distributed them to a number of gullible accomplices to collect signatures. Never had there been, and perhaps never again has there been, such excitement on the Russell High campus. Teachers were peering out their doors at clusters of chattering students in the halls and on the campus signing the petitions. In the middle of the afternoon all students were summoned to an assembly in the auditorium. Mr. West informed the hushed but aroused gathering that they had been "following the wrong leadership," that school policy was set by the Board of Education and that there should be no more petitions. He neither stated nor asked who were the instigators in this case.

The assembly was dismissed and we all returned to our classrooms. At the end of that period, however, Alan and I got together and decided to take our indignation to the principal. Mr. West received us politely and listened respectfully to our protests. He defended the segregation as a reasonable method of controlling the student body and assuring a good educational environment. Then he pointed out that we were minors under the control of our parents and that the school operated *in locus parentis,* or something like that. We had not studied Latin, but we interpreted this loosely to mean, "We tell you what to do and you'll do what you are told."

We thanked Mr. West for explaining it to us and took our leave. We continued to feign indignation, but intellectually I decided that Mr. West was right. As I write this sixty years later, the newspapers are filled with stories of shootings, drugs, sex and unwed mothers in the schools. My conscience bothers me with the thought that Alan and I may have contributed to the changes that brought this about.

By my senior year I was involved in a number of school activities that I thoroughly enjoyed. As a member of the school newspaper staff, I attended all the football games and wrote play-by-play descriptions for the paper. I was a captain in the R.O.T.C., which gave me the privilege of wearing a sporty cap with a bill and having a "sponsor" for the R.O.T.C.-day parade. This posed a problem. Most of the officers had their girlfriends as sponsors and some had their mothers. I had no girlfriend, and my mother would have moved back to the farm before she would have been involved in such activity.

As the deadline approached for selecting a sponsor I became more and more apprehensive. I was too stupid to realize that the girls considered being a sponsor a great honor and, despite the fact that I was far removed from the "in" group, most any girl not already "taken" would have accepted an invitation from me. A very pretty girl, Edna Reynolds, sat to my right in one of my classes, and I looked at her as often as possible without making a complete fool of myself. When her eyes met mine she would always flash a friendly smile. Eventually I worked up the courage to ask her if she would be my sponsor. She said, "Yes," immediately and was obviously genuinely pleased.

The senior prom followed the R.O.T.C. parade. I had not planned to attend and didn't think how this would affect my "sponsor." Not having a car, I could not take her home after the parade, so she rode home with her parents. I am still embarrassed when I think about that situation, because I suspect her heart was broken—not over me, but because of the social humiliation. Considering that I was such a social idiot, it is amazing that I was named in the school yearbook as the "Most Intellectual Boy," and I was one of ten honor graduates. I was not the valedictorian; that honor was reserved for "Most Likely to Succeed," Fred Wilson. But during the graduation ceremony I had to thread my way through the other students, down the risers on which we were seated, four times to receive awards. The third and fourth times I made that awkward descent, the applause was exuberant. I was overwhelmed by this unexpected acclamation.

24
Post Graduation

The glow from my fifteen minutes of fame ended the day after graduation. One of my awards was a scholarship to William and Mary College but it covered only a small part of actual expenses. I had no work experience that might help me find part-time work, and I was totally ignorant as to what was involved in living away from home. So the idea of going to college was quickly abandoned. The time had come to find a job, but jobs were not easily found. I like to think that I searched diligently, but there is embarrassing evidence suggesting otherwise.

Shortly after graduation, Floyd, who was a scoutmaster, invited me to come to Birmingham and give a magic show at an awards ceremony for his troop. As added enticement, he told me Oretta was there living with him and Aunt Kate while looking for a job.

The magic show was at the Vinesville Baptist Church and there were well over one hundred in attendance. This was my first "big" show, but it went quite well with a lot of applause and laughter—until my grand finale. This was many years before television, but my ending trick was called *The Television Card Trick*. A selected card vanished and was supposed to reappear instantaneously between two plates of glass. Because of a mechanical breakdown, it didn't appear. Only a magician who has had a similar experience can appreciate my feeling of humiliation. Fortunately, however, I had prudently memorized "ad libs" to cover such situations and managed a lame conclusion to my act. After the show, flattering comments from many of the audience considerably soothed my bruised ego. I was surprised and delighted when a prosperous-looking young man introduced himself and told me we were in the first grade together. It was Lawrence George.

Oretta and I got along pretty well. One evening we walked to a new "roadhouse" a few blocks away on Bessemer Boulevard where we had a Coca-Cola and listened to the juke box. Another evening we sat on the front steps and talked after everyone else had gone to bed. There was some "sparking," but hardly enough to set off a fire alarm. However, it lit my fire enough that Oretta was pretty constantly on my mind long after I got back to East Point.

Later in the summer, I talked Leon into driving over to Birmingham in his 1932 Chevrolet. Big mistake. I think we spent two nights. One of those nights I found myself talking with Floyd while Leon and Oretta went for a ride in his Chevrolet. I can't say that my heart was broken—it continued to beat—but it hurt for a long time. Leon remained my friend, and I continued to get reports on Oretta from Floyd from time to time, but I never saw her again.

In November, 1941, an employment agency found a job for me with Wilson & Company Meat Packers in Atlanta. For the first several weeks a substantial portion of my salary went to the employment agency. That salary was $15.00 for five and one-half days. During the week my job required that I go to the First National Bank, a distance of one mile, to make the daily deposit. The company paid me fifteen cents to cover the cost of two trolley "tokens". An example of our Depression-age thrift is the fact that I walked one way, stopping in route to eat lunch, to save seven and one-half cents. Of course this was a significant amount in those days; my lunch—a meat, a drink and two vegetables—cost twenty-five cents.

While I was in high school my usual attire was my R.O.T.C. uniform or pants, shirt and "zipper jacket." But shortly before graduation I had someway managed to buy a suit from the O.P.O. Clothing Store. "O.P.O." stood for "One Price Only," which was $19.95. Because I was so tall and skinny—six feet, two-and-one-half inches, one hundred fifty pounds—ready-made suits did not fit me very well. One of my jokes when doing magic was to say my suit was tailor-made, then add "Of course it wasn't made for me."

After I went to work, as soon as I saved enough money, I went to a tailor in downtown Atlanta and had a suit made. I don't know that it helped my appearance very much, but it did help my self-confidence. Also, several times a week I walked or rode the trolley from work to the Y.M.C.A.* in downtown Atlanta. I ran on the inside track and swam when there was no one else in the pool. I was too self-conscious to swim with others because it was customary at that time to swim nude in that male-only environment. When weather permitted I sunbathed on the roof of the building. I was still very much a callow youth, but felt somewhat less awkward and unattractive.

It was around this time that I met my Secret Love. We met at the Atlanta Public Library, which was a block or so from the Y.M.C.A. She was an absolutely beautiful

---

*Young Men's Christian Association.

girl, who was engaged to marry a boy who had been drafted. She worked in Atlanta and lived as a roomer with a family friend. She was quite lonely and she saw me as a "safe" companion while she remained faithful to her fiancé. When I asked her to go to a movie at the Fox Theater she agreed only after telling me about her betrothed and emphasizing that we could only be "friends."

Perhaps because of that understanding, we were amazingly congenial. I began meeting her every Friday for a hamburger at the Krystal, across the street from the Greyhound bus station, before she caught the bus to go home to Douglasville for the weekend. Once or twice during the week we would go to a movie or meet at the library or just walk around downtown Atlanta. When the weather was cold we sometimes walked in the Peachtree Arcade, which was a precursor of the modern mall—a gallery of shops opening onto a courtyard with the whole thing covered by a glass roof.

She told me how pleasant it was to have someone she could be with and not feel "threatened." I assured her I had no desire to become involved romantically, particularly since I expected to be drafted any day, and I really didn't like her that much, anyway. She laughed and said she didn't like me very much either, so it was a perfect arrangement.

The library had a labyrinth of bookshelves, and one day in one of the hidden aisles I kissed her. Apparently she got to thinking about her real boyfriend, for she responded with an ardor like I had never experienced. Realizing that matters were becoming complicated, we promised not to do that sort of thing again. But we did. Neither my family nor hers nor any of our friends knew we were seeing each other. When we met there were almost always other people around but it was as if we entered a secret world of our own.

The Selective Service Act was passed in 1940 and by the time Japan bombed Pearl Harbor (December 7, 1941), the draft was in full force. W.T. and Freeman were called early in 1942. T went into the army March 4, 1942, but because of an irregular heart beat, Freeman was turned down. Ironically, his civilian job, running an open-cab, coal-burning crane in weather ranging from freezing to 104 degrees, was harder physically than most armed forces jobs.

Leon talked me into joining the State Guard with him the summer of 1942. We belonged to a Medical Unit and met twice a week in a large building in College Park, where we practiced close order drill and studied first aid. It was essentially the same sort of training I'd had in the R.O.T.C. for four years. I hated it. And after a few weeks Leon, who had been threatening to join the Marines for months, finally did so to protect his reputation. So I had to go to the twice-weekly guard meetings alone. I was happy when my draft notice came.

February 3, 1943, I was inducted at Fort McPherson and (I'm not making this up) I was put on KP* before I was even sworn in. The next day I stood around naked with a bunch of similarly clad men for such fun things as forming a circle, facing outward and bending over while the doctors checked for whatever it was they were checking for. Each of us also had a psychological exam, which mainly consisted of the unambiguous question, "Do you

*Kitchen Police.

like girls?" Any ambiguity in the reply assured an immediate return to civilian life.

After several days of tests and examinations, when every trace of privacy had been obliterated, I was given the ironic title "Private Stanfield" and a week off to get my affairs in order before reporting back for duty. I got the date mixed up and reported in a day late. But I guess I got credit for the KP served before I was sworn in, for there was no punishment for being AWOL.* The only repercussion was that I was separated from other draftees from East Point and found myself among a bunch of Yankees and a few guys from Alabama headed for Ft. Sill, Oklahoma.

We stayed at Ft. McPherson about ten days before boarding a troop train for Ft. Sill. During that time we were allowed visitors at night. Some of my sisters, Floyd, and a couple of girls from Russell High (Ora Jean Porter and Eva Mae Goen) visited me. But I must confess the most poignant visits were from my Secret Love. We knew ours was a hopeless relationship, but we sat on park benches on the fort grounds, vowed our love and shared our sorrow at having to part. The last night she visited, I walked with her outside the Main Gate where there was a sheltered bench for waiting for a trolley. After she left I made my way back to the barracks in agony. Never have I felt such melancholy as that night as I lay in my bunk and the bugler sounded *Taps*.

---

*Absent without leave.

25
Fort Sill

I think my army aptitude tests indicated that I was exceptionally qualified for KP. On the troop train to Ft. Sill I had the honor of being selected again for that duty. Washing dishes and carrying food from the kitchen car to the troops relieved the monotony of the two-day trip and gave me access to a ten-gallon dispenser filled with pineapple juice. I was sick as a dog by the time we reached Ft. Sill, and I couldn't stand pineapple juice for several years after.

Field Artillery training was not so bad except for the unaccustomed cold, frequently near zero. We were outside most of the time. We had wood-burning stoves in the barracks, but could build fires only at night. When we had inside classes during the day, there was no heat. I had been weakened by diarrhea from drinking too much pineapple juice and had a terrible cold, which steadily worsened until one day during "cannoneer's hop" I coughed up blood. I went on sick call the next morning and was put into the dispensary.

The second day I was in the dispensary, an orderly yelled out from the other end of the room, "Stanfield. Telephone. Long distance."

In those days, a long-distance phone call was an extraordinary event. This was one of two I received during my three years in the army. Under the curious eyes of the other patients, in a hospital shirt that barely reached my hips, I walked the two miles from my bunk to the phone at the other end of the barracks. It was Mother responding to a telepathic message that had told her I was sick. Mothers are uncanny. I was miserable, but assured her I was okay. Apparently the medic on duty heard me, for he ordered me back to my unit the next morning even though I felt worse than when I came in. I thought I wouldn't live through the day, and was almost delirious with fever when I got into my bunk that night. During the night my fever "broke" and I sweated so profusely that my long underwear was literally soaked. But the next morning I awoke feeling fine.

There was no one else from Georgia in my unit at Ft. Sill, but there were three men from Alabama, all from the vicinity of Anniston: Joe Stanfield (no relation), Lauris T. Jones, and Dozier Shaw. We usually sat together in the mess hall and sometimes went together to Lawton on weekend passes. Joe, who was a few years older than I, had married a short time before being drafted. He and I commiserated with each other; he bemoaning how much he missed his new wife and I confiding my anguish regarding my Secret Love.

Mail call was the high point of every day. Dozier Shaw got multiple letters, so much so that I wrote a poem with the lines:

Damn that grinning gargoyle who,
At mail call doesn't stop at two,
   Or three or four, but takes the whole dern lot
Of "S's" then looks up and says,
Is that all you have that begins with "S?"
   As if he hadn't hit the "S" jackpot!

Gleaning humor from the discomfort, boredom, and homesickness was the only way we endured. That and letters from home. I got a reasonable amount of mail from Floyd, my family and friends. And occasionally a letter from my Secret Love. I blushed with embarrassment (and pride) when the mail clerk sometimes held such letters up for all to see the lip imprint she sealed them with. After reading them repeatedly, I destroyed her letters but I cut the flap with her lip print from an envelope and kept it in my billfold with her picture. She had sent me a color photo, a rarity at that time, and had written on the back, "I love you, you old sweet monkey!" Hardly the soaring poetry of Elizabeth Barrett Browning's *How do I love thee* . . . but equally beautiful and endearing beyond measure to me.

Deep down, I suppose I knew from the start the "Dear John letter" would come. But that didn't make it any easier when it did. She wrote that her fiancé was coming home on furlough before going overseas and wanted to be married at once. She reminded me we had agreed to be "just friends." She said she meant it when she said she loved me, but that it would be better if we did not write each other anymore. I was so distraught I couldn't think straight. Angrily, I jotted down a reply to the effect that "first come, first served" was a good policy in business but not in love. I lay awake regretting it all night, then mailed another letter the next day begging her to forgive my stupidity. I never heard from her again.

26
A.S.T.P.

I was so despondent and depressed that it was almost a life-saving event when my commanding officer suggested that I apply for Officer Candidate School. April 26, 1943, I was tentatively accepted. In preparation, I was "pulled" from regular training to attend some special refresher classes in mathematics. A few days later I was informed that the O.C.S. had been canceled because there was no requirement for additional artillery officers. However, I could apply for a new Army Specialized Training Program under which "high I.Q." personnel were enrolled as students at various universities, from which they would graduate as second lieutenants.

June 4, 1943, after about ten days of exams and aptitude tests at the Oklahoma A & M College, Stillwater, I enrolled at the University of Arkansas in Fayetteville. I had anticipated that I would be approved for language studies and eventually end up in Army Intelligence. However, I had not taken any foreign languages in high school but had taken "Electric Shop." Also I had tinkered with radios. Probably because I knew the difference between a volt and a watt, the tests indicated an aptitude for Electrical Engineering. So my courses were calculus, chemistry, physics, etc., preparatory for that profession.

The A.S.T.P. schedule was such that we had little time to think about unhappiness or lost loves. We slept in student dormitories, five to a room, and we attended classes under the University professors. But we were segregated from the civilian students, mostly girls, and activities were stringently regimented. Beginning with reveille at 5:30, we took care of personal hygiene, made our bunks, and cleaned our rooms before beginning classes, which included military subjects and physical activities. We marched to and from the classrooms and the cafeteria, ending the day in a supervised study hall from 6:00 to 8:00 P.M. Most students continued to study in their rooms until lights out at ten. On Saturdays we were dismissed at 3:00 P.M. until time for study hall at six Sunday afternoon. (Bee has a letter that I wrote to Rebecca in which I complained that a new commandant had changed the Saturday dismissal time to 6:00 P.M. and imposed Sunday morning reveille.) On Sunday mornings most of us did our laundry, hanging underwear and socks on lines strung back and forth across the room.

Despite the accelerated pace, I enjoyed classes and had little difficulty—except in chemistry. Even there I managed to make decent grades. I used to say I made "straight A's," but after running across an old transcript I changed that to "straight grades," a phrase I learned from Bee's husband, Bill Higgins. In nine months we earned credits equivalent to two years of "regular" college.

There was little extracurricular time, therefore little extracurricular activity. When we were dismissed Saturday afternoon many, if not most, of the men took off immediately to see girlfriends or otherwise entertain themselves in the town of Fayetteville. Most did not have my frugal upbringing. I always ate Saturday evening cold-cuts at the school cafeteria before walking down to the Fayetteville movie theater. Although my classmates were all quite congenial, I spent a considerable part of my free time alone. Occasionally I showed a magic trick to my roommates and, having studied palm reading enough to sound as though I knew what I was doing, one day I read their palms. Amazingly, this malarkey was so fascinating that for a week or so afterward guys were coming by from all over the dormitory for me to read their palms.

One of the students, Mike Michaelson, had been involved in some sort of show business as a civilian, and he came up with the idea of having the A.S.T.P. put on a variety show in the school auditorium. Because of the palm reading, my "fame" as a magician had reached Mike, so he asked me to perform in the show. The entire student body, including civilians, was invited so there was an audience of about five hundred. I had only small "parlor" tricks, so my act was more talk than magic. However, perhaps because people were not so saturated with entertainment in those days, my little tricks and topical humor were received with tremendous laughter and applause.

A week or so later, Mike got me to perform in another show for a group of senior citizens (then called "old people"). There was no pay, of course, but there was a fringe benefit: Mike's girlfriend and her girlfriend, Gretchen Stockford, were at the show. They definitely were not senior citizens. We went to their apartment afterward and Gretchen helped me get my Secret Love off my mind. (Considering the lifestyles of young people these days, I should explain that she did this by vivacious conversation, a bit of flattery about my performance and just a touch of flirtation.)

I dated Gretchen two or three times, then one Friday I telephoned to ask if I could see her the following day. She informed me that she already had a date with a lieutenant. He had sung to her the *cutest* new song called "Mairzy Doats" and he was the *cutest* thing. I knew I couldn't compete with a lieutenant, particularly one who could sing, so I didn't call Gretchen again. However, I did learn all the words to *Mairzy Doats,* anticipating the time when I would have my own gold bars.

Sometime later Mike organized another A.S.T.P. variety show and again asked me to perform. The show was scheduled for a Saturday night. That morning I received a telegram from the Red Cross telling me that Pat had been in an accident and was in critical condition. They said they were requesting an emergency furlough for me and that my orders should come through shortly. After several torturous hours the orders were received, and I caught a Greyhound bus. Having a long layover in Memphis, I decided to try hitchhiking from there. Soldiers routinely hitchhiked then, and it wasn't long before a doctor headed for Birmingham picked me up. To conserve tires and gasoline, President Roosevelt had ordered a thirty-five-mile-per-hour national speed limit but, after asking me to watch out for cops, the good doctor drove up to eighty miles per hour on that winding two-lane highway. Making it more exciting, he had a nervous tic that caused him to jerk his head sideways two or three times a minute.

I felt considerable relief when he let me out at the bus station in Birmingham. Buses were always crowded to capacity, but soldiers went to the head of the line. I managed to get on a bus to Atlanta, but that was before the death of chivalry, so ladies still got priority on seats. I stood up, hanging on the baggage rack. We had traveled what seemed to me to be about fifteen minutes when the driver announced we were stopping for a rest break in Anniston. I had slept for two hours standing up. About three hours later we arrived in Atlanta. I was in pretty good shape because I had got a seat after the Anniston stop.

I took a streetcar to the hospital, where Pat was still in critical condition, still unconscious. Two days earlier, she and two of her seventh-grade girlfriends, Ann Reeves and Christine Thomas, had attended a meeting of the "Girls Auxiliary," a Baptist Sunday School group, at Russell High School. Ann's mother was driving them home. When she crossed the railroad racks adjacent to the school, she stopped before entering Main Street. Her car had not quite cleared the tracks and was hit by a freight train. Ann was seriously hurt and Christine was killed instantly. Mrs. Reeves was thrown into Main Street, where she was run over by an automobile. Frightened and confused, the driver backed up and ran over her again, but miraculously, she survived. After the ambulance crews had loaded the survivors and were preparing to leave, someone heard a moaning sound and discovered Pat in a ditch, her face buried in water, about thirty feet beyond the crossing. She had a fractured skull, brain hemorrhaging and two or three broken vertebrae.

Two days before my leave was to end, Pat regained consciousness, but remained delirious, singing snatches of songs and counting out loud "One, two, three, four, five, etc.," then repeating it over and over. W.T. was also home on emergency leave and, at the doctor's suggestion, we wired for five-day extensions. He and I or some other members of the family maintained a somber vigil for several days before Pat began to improve. She was still in the hospital when T and I returned to our units, but within another week or so she was home.

In those days automobile liability insurance was a rarity and, in any event, no insurance companies were involved. Even though there had been no guard or automatic gates at the crossing, practically adjoining the school grounds, no one even thought of suing for damages. Southern Railway voluntarily paid all Pat's medical expenses and Daddy thanked them for their generosity.

Pat recovered completely from the ordeal, but I haven't yet forgiven her for causing me to miss performing at the A.S.T.P. variety show. The fact that I did not become a famous vaudeville star can be traced directly back to that event.

Meanwhile, in Europe and in the Pacific, America was fighting a war. As I later discovered, the establishment of the A.S.T.P. had involved a political battle from the start. By January, 1944, the war was not going well and the military leaders were looking for replacements for the thousands of dead and wounded. We began to hear rumors that the A.S.T.P. and its Navy counterpart would be dissolved. A number of us at the University of Arkansas already felt vaguely uncomfortable reading news of the war, seeing patriotic war movies and, closer to home, seeing the air cadets at the university marching along lustily singing, "Off we go into the wild, blue yonder." We marched to such rousing ditties as *I've Got Sixpence* or *The Rootin' Tootin' Spider*.

So when the rumors began that the A.S.T.P. might end about twenty of us applied to become air cadets. One fine morning a charter bus took us to the air force base in Muskogee, Oklahoma, for admission tests. After an orientation session, we went through two days of rigorous mental and physical examinations. I was concerned that my height and my stick-figure physique might work against me, but met all the criteria and was accepted along with most of the other applicants. Orders were issued transferring us to "Army Air Corps, Unassigned," and we were told to return to our units to await assignments. During our last meal in the air base mess hall, which was like a fine restaurant, we watched through plate glass windows as the trainees practiced takeoffs and landings. I had never even driven an automobile, but I visualized myself at the controls of one of those planes roaring off into the sky.

Our charter bus driver, who had spent two nights in a Muskogee hotel, picked us up for the return to Fayetteville. After driving about thirty miles he remembered that he had left his billfold under his pillow at the hotel and turned around. We were so elated that we were now in the Air Corps that we didn't even grumble. When he emerged from the hotel holding his billfold high in the air we gave a rousing hurrah. Back at the University we were in high spirits as we continued our usual routine.

After a few weeks the formal announcement came that the A.S.T.P. was being dissolved. In our final formation on the parade ground we were told that all personnel would be transferred immediately to infantry divisions. Those who were "Air Corps, Unassigned" were told to remain in formation after the others were dismissed. We were informed that we would be transferred along with the others, but orders assigning us to Air Corps units would be forthcoming.

27
Camp Maxey

The troop train sat on a sidetrack in the middle of downtown Fayetteville. We marched in formation from the University, and it felt like a funeral march. Most of the townspeople were gathered to see us off. There were hugs and kisses and tears from one end of the train to the other. If Gretchen was there I didn't see her, but Mike's girlfriend tore herself away from him long enough to give me a goodbye kiss. It had to last me a long time.

Camp Maxey was a sea of white two-story barracks stretching as far as we could see when our train pulled in. "Sea" is a simile only to describe size and sameness; it was dusty and dry with no suggestion of water anywhere near. (I later learned there was a lake on the grounds, but actually don't remember ever seeing it.)

Including our group from Arkansas, there were about three thousand A.S.T.P. students arriving at about the same time. As a part of our processing each man was interviewed by an officer or non-com sitting behind a desk with our individual records before him. He carefully considered our qualifications and aptitudes before assigning us to an infantry company for twelve weeks of accelerated training in the art of killing with rifle and bayonet. My interviewer noticed that I was "Air Corps, Unassigned" and assured me confidently that my records should "catch up with me shortly." In a spirit of cooperation, I agreed to go ahead with the infantry training anyway. I was assigned to Company G, 393rd. Infantry.

Including my high school R.O.T.C., I had already gone through basic training three times so I had pretty well learned that phosgene gas smells like new-mown hay and how to apply a tourniquet to stop the flow of blood. But I was introduced for the first time to such things as assembling a model M-1 rifle in the dark, crawling under barbed wire and live ammunition, running while wearing a gas mask, and making ferocious noises while lunging with a fixed bayonet. (The sergeant told me "Take that!" wouldn't do.)

The officers, non-coms and enlisted men in the 99th when we arrived had been with the division since its activation in 1942 at Camp Van Dorn, a mosquito-infested, woebegone camp in the swamps of Mississippi. They looked on us from the A.S.T.P. as "smart-ass college boys" and treated us accordingly. This attitude, plus the push to get us ready to ship out as quickly as possible, created an almost unbearable atmosphere. We were hurried and harassed constantly. We had to take care of personal matters, such as shining our shoes and cleaning our rifles, at eight or nine o'clock at night. In a letter to mother dated April 10, 1944, I wrote,

> *It's Monday night. Guess I better shave and get to bed. First place I've been where we didn't get up at the same time every morning. Here it's sometimes as late as 5:45 and sometimes as early as 4:30. That's what time we got up this morning, and I think we're supposed to again tomorrow. I don't mind so much, though. It gives me just that much more time to enjoy this <u>wonderful</u> life in the infantry.*

Humor still helped make life easier and I frequently composed rhymes, usually humorous, during boring chores. One night while we were "in the field" I was on guard duty and (in my mind) wrote:

A stalwart, stately sentinel, I,
And as I walk the hours by
I chant this stirring, valiant song:
There's none so tall, so brave, so strong!

The hours go by and like a boulder,
My gun grows heavy on my shoulder.
Suppose that last small point we waive,
But still there's none so tall, so brave.

Late the hour and dark the night,
The bordering woods are deadly quiet.
A screech owl shrieks its eerie call;
Well, anyway, there's none so tall!

I had only one close associate during that period. He was also from A.S.T.P., very intellectual, read classical literature, liked classical music and was obviously somewhat "upper class." We commiserated with each other about the horrible conditions and went to movies a number of times when the lines were not too long at the post theater. Strangely, I can't even remember his name.

Orders transferring me to an Air Corps unit never arrived. But apparently there was a need for artillery personnel and someone checking my M.O.S.* noticed that I

*Military Occupation Symbol.

had been trained in that field. Orders came down transferring me to Battery B 371st Field Artillery. I gratefully packed my barracks bag and walked to the 371st barracks. The only time I ever went back to Company G was to try to collect two dollars I had loaned to a fellow private. I didn't collect the two dollars, but a sergeant told me that it was too bad I'd transferred because I had been slated for promotion to sergeant. That did not have the intended effect of making me regret my transfer.

Life in the artillery continued to be strenuous, but much less miserable than in the infantry. We were continuously on bivouac or maneuvers, preparing for imminent shipment overseas. In June, 1944, we traveled by motor convoy to Fort Hood, Texas, for maneuvers which lasted about one week, during which we lived in the field under simulated battle conditions. When we were "strafed" by roaring, low-flying aircraft I experienced renewed resentment that I was still awaiting transfer to the Air Corp.

Our 105mm Howitzers were pulled with 2 1/2-ton trucks. As a part of our training every man was required to drive one of those trucks. Out in an open field, each man in turn took the driver's seat with a sergeant sitting beside him telling him to turn, back up, "double clutch", etc. so that he would be able to drive the vehicle in an emergency. When my turn came, it *was* an emergency. I had never driven a car of any sort. With gears grinding viciously, I managed to get the truck in gear. With the engine racing, I let out the clutch. The truck leaped forward. I jammed on the brake. The engine sounded as if it were mortally wounded, but roared back to life when I pushed in the clutch. I tried again. The truck lurched and bucked like a wild bronco, bouncing the sergeant back and forth. Fearing for his life, he invoked the name of God. But not in a very prayerful manner. He decided we would skip the "double-clutching" instructions altogether, and suggested that the army would be better off if I never got behind a steering wheel again.

My driving lesson had occurred a month or so earlier, but I was reminded of it and learned the importance of well-trained drivers when we headed back to Camp Maxey after maneuvers.

To guide motor convoys, soldiers called "markers" were stationed at intervals along the route. I was on marker duty on the return trip to Camp Maxey and, for that reason, was riding in a truck with other markers instead of with my gun crew. There were eight of us, four on each of the side benches in the body of the truck. We started around a left curve and, even though we did not seem to be going very fast, the driver lost control and the truck turned over, off the road and down a steep bank.

Those of us on the left bench were catapulted through the air, seeming to move in slow motion, and landed at the foot of the bank beyond the capsized truck. Those on the right bench also escaped the truck, but the supply trailer we were pulling rolled over on Joe Uhr, who had been seated directly across from me at the rear end of the truck. We did what we could to comfort him. Someone offered him water from a canteen, but someone else remembered that water should not be given because of possible internal injuries. We had recently been issued packets of the new wonder drug, penicillin, and trying desperately to think what we could do to help Joe, I poured the powdered medicine on an ugly gash on his arm.

One other soldier was somewhat less seriously injured. The medics arrived and rushed him and Joe to the nearest hospital. The rest of us, who suffered no significant injuries, were loaded onto another vehicle to continue to Camp Maxey. The less seriously injured man was transferred to Lawson General Hospital in Atlanta, where I assume he made a complete recovery. But Joe died from internal injuries the next day.

Captain Frois selected me to accompany Joe's body to his hometown of Springfield, Missouri. It was an overnight trip so I rode in a Pullman car, which was a unique experience. After the porter made up berths some of the civilian passengers went to the bathroom, dressed in pajamas and robes and returned to their compartments. I had no robe and, since I slept in my underwear, I was in a quandary as to how I was to retire in my upper berth. Finally I crawled into the space fully clothed and clumsily removed my shoes, coat, pants and shirt. The next morning I even more clumsily put them back on.

I stood by ceremoniously as Joe's body was transferred to the hearse in Springfield. With utmost courtesy and consideration, his family took me to their home, where I spent two nights before the funeral. Most of the men being away at war, several of Joe's female cousins and his girlfriend treated me royally, driving me around town, telling me about Joe's life and asking questions about the army. They were particularly interested in my experiences at the University of Arkansas, where several of their acquaintances were students. After months of crude living conditions with only male companions, being chauffeured around in luxurious automobiles by beautiful girls was a heavenly experience. One of them, the winner of a local beauty contest, drove me to see her life-size photograph on a cardboard cut-out in front of a public building with the caption "Miss Springfield." Remembering the reason for my trip, my conscience bothered me because I was enjoying it so much. I declined an invitation for one pleasure trip in order to spend time with Mr.

and Mrs. Uhr, but, even though they were extremely nice to me, I sensed that they were more comfortable being alone or with their family. I corresponded with Mrs. Uhr and Joe's girlfriend, Martha Stapleton, for a year or so after Joe's funeral.

28
Shipping Out

A few weeks after I got back from Springfield I went home on a two-week furlough. With W.T. and all my male friends "gone to war," and with no girlfriend, my furlough was a rather melancholy time. I made a trip to Tennessee, but my cousins Neal and Ray were away in the service. Uncle Will and Aunt Lydia had moved into town, where they were custodians at the county jail. Jean and Jo, who now lived in Nashville, seldom visited. Aunt Lydia cooked for the prisoners and it was rumored that some of the town deadbeats deliberately got themselves arrested to enjoy her cooking. Uncle Will was sick with the beginning of a throat cancer that was to take his life a few years later. I was still brooding with bittersweet memories of my Secret Love, so the return to Camp Maxey was almost welcome. But shortly after I got there I wrote home:

Well, Hell has claimed her own again,
And now we start to groan again.
Leaving there was rough you know,
I sure did hate to see me go!

Preparations were underway for going overseas. After more than a year in the army, I had finally been promoted to PFC, but no one asked my advice about anything and my participation in these preparations was minimal. The main thing I remember about getting ready to "ship out" is having our helmets and helmet liners painted. We had to have this done on our own time, that is after we were dismissed for the day, before a specified date. The paint station was a mile or so from our barracks, and I suppose the helmets and liners for the entire division were painted at that one spot, for I remember having to go there more than once because of long lines. They had an air compressor and a paint spray gun, which was fascinating to me because I had never before seen either of those items. Apparently they used quick-drying olive drab paint because I don't remember having to wait for it to dry.

After all helmets had been painted and, I suppose, a few other tasks completed, we boarded a troop train September 15 and headed north. Since the 99th had trained in hot, muggy Mississippi and Louisiana and in hot, dry Texas, many of us assumed we would be going to the tropical South Pacific or to the desert region of Africa. So it seemed strange to be traveling north. We crossed into Canada and turned east, still not knowing our destination. I was aware that French was spoken in portions of Canada, but it still seemed incredible, when we passed through Quebec, that there were cities so near our borders where all the signs were in a foreign language.

September 19 we reached our destination, Camp Miles Standish, near Taunton, Massachusetts. We spent about two weeks there while the powers that be worked out the logistics for transporting trainloads of equipment and 50,000 men overseas. I rode a bus to Boston on a 24-hour pass and spent the day walking around, using a tourist map to locate historic sites. The only one I remember is a park famous as the location for "soapbox" speakers. But there were no soapboxes and no speakers while I was there. Late in the afternoon, I saw a sign in front of a restaurant advertising a floorshow that featured a magician. Never having been to a "nightclub" restaurant of this type, I went in somewhat hesitantly. The waitress was quite attentive, perhaps because there were only a few customers. When she served my meal I asked her what time the floorshow started. I think it was 9:30 or some such ridiculously late hour, so I left without seeing the show and caught the bus back to Camp Miles Standish.

Carrying all our worldly possessions in duffel bags and barracks bags, we rode a day train into the Boston harbor. It was wet and miserably cold as we made our way, like a procession of worker ants, from the train to a subterranean dock area with huge columns supporting the pier. Either the Red Cross or the Salvation Army gave each of us a doughnut and a cup of coffee. I leaned against a column to help support my duffel bag and bed roll as I ate. Our barracks bags, which had been marked in accordance with strict instructions, were piled on the dock to be stored in the hold of the ship. We had been warned to keep necessary personal items in our duffel bags because we would not see the barracks bags again until we landed.

As an officer called individual names and checked us off, we trudged up a narrow, steep gangplank. From the deck, we descended on ladders into the belly of the ship, where hammocks were stacked head to foot (eight high, I believe) with about eighteen-inch aisles between the rows. I threw my bedroll and duffel bag into a bunk, fourth from the bottom, to stake my claim, then went to find the "head," the nautical term for "latrine."

I don't remember how much more exploring of the ship we did that night, but I know it wasn't much because we were dead tired from the day's activities. We wedged ourselves into the hammocks, which were so close together it was barely possible to turn over without touching the one above. In this dungeon-like atmosphere I found myself visualizing a torpedo bursting in followed by gushing water. But fortunately sleep came quickly. Sometime during the night a rumbling noise and continuous vibration awakened me as the ship got under way. On deck the next morning we could see nothing but water and sky in all directions. We were in a convoy of six ships, but none of the others was within view. Eventually I learned that our convoy was "shadowed" by a German submarine, but we were never fired on. I also learned that those submarines had sunk about 400 American ships up to that time. Sleep might not have come so easily in that cramped hammock if I had known this while we were at sea.

Many of the men were so seasick that they seldom got out of their bunks and the smell of vomit was commonplace. While I was "woozy" for the entire voyage, I never became sick and never lost my appetite. We had two meals per day, served cafeteria style, and we stood at high tables to eat. When the sea was rough this added a new dimension to the dining experience. Because so many were too sick to eat, there was ample food and it was considerably more palatable than regular army chow.

Once at sea we were finally told we were going to England. We were given lectures regarding the English money system and customs different from our own, including differences in the use of the English language. A most memorable example was the warning that we should not get too excited if we understood a British lass to be asking us to perform a very personal service, because she probably would be simply asking us to telephone the next morning to wake her up. Except for this English orientation and daily calisthenics we had little supervised activity and were free to read, wander the decks or just lie in the sun.

Knowing England was only a staging area, the most common phrase in our conversation was, "It won't be long now." We had no radio, but we had daily broadcasts on the ship speaker system. This was mostly music, but there were some special features. There was a sort of broadcast studio, and a couple of times I did magic "on the air," describing the tricks as I showed them to the broadcast crew. Of course I boasted to the listeners that they would not be able to "see how I did it."

We had left Boston September 29. October 10 we landed at Liverpool. Other elements of the 99th landed at various ports and then went to a number of different staging areas. We went to a British army camp, Camp D-6, near Dorchester. The coaches of the train we rode from Liverpool looked like miniatures compared with American counterparts. When we crowded in with our barracks bags there was hardly room to stretch our legs but, fortunately, the ride to Dorchester took only two or three hours. The camp was quite comfortable. We were amused by the fact that the toilet facilities were in a building completely separate from the showers and each commode was in a private stall. We were accustomed to combined showers and latrines where the commodes were side-by-side in one open area.

We resumed a full military schedule at Camp D-6, with the emphasis on extended marches. These were made along the rural roads and were not bad because of the pleasant surroundings—fields of green farmland separated by hedgerows and picturesque houses with thick thatch roofs. Only the food kept our stay in England from being rather enjoyable. But the food was terrible. The main staple was mutton, "goat stew," which I found inedible even when drowned in catsup.

One weekend I went on pass to London along with my crew chief, Sergeant Lloyd Cannady, who had become a good friend. Our train stopped at a station about midway, and we got off to buy a cup of coffee at a railside snack bar. When I asked for sugar, the girl behind the counter responded in a very haughty British accent, "Don't you know there's a war on!" I thought, *No, I'm just over here on a vacation trip.* But I didn't say that because I didn't think of it until I started drinking that unsweetened coffee.

In London we got a cheap room in Piccadilly Circus at a USO facility, then set out walking to explore the town. Perhaps "town" is not the best word to describe London, even as it was in 1944. It was a huge city. I had a particular interest in seeing Dickens' Olde Curiousity Shoppe, which we did find. But we didn't see much else other than commercial sites and bombed-out buildings. When night came the town was completely blacked out. There was no air raid that night, the sirens were silent, so there was a considerable amount of pedestrian traffic. As we crossed the street at an intersection we almost collided with two girls walking toward us. One of them shined her "torch" (flashlight) in our faces. Or maybe it was only in Lloyd's face, for they responded to our apology in such a friendly fashion that we changed directions and began walking with them.

Fortunately, (perhaps at the time I would have said unfortunately) Margaret and Pauline turned out to be very nice girls. I assume there was a full moon that night, for we could see reasonably well despite the blackout.

They showed us a number of tourist sites in the area, but I can remember only Lord Nelson's statue, Trafalgar Square and, I believe, Serpentine Lake. We took them to a restaurant, up a flight of stairs directly from the sidewalk, where we had a reasonably good dinner—no meat. We then found a bench in a nearby park, where we exchanged addresses (and a few kisses) before we boarded the "Tube" to take them home. (At that time the VCR had not been invented, but romantic encounters were often put on "fast forward" because of the press of time and the uncertainty of the future.) We left them at their station and caught the next train back to town.

Margaret had given me her torch to hold and I had forgotten to give it back. I knew she would find it almost impossible to replace, so I left it at a USO station with the request that they hold it for her to pick up. There was no way to telephone her, but I wrote her a letter at the first opportunity telling her where to find her torch. Margaret wrote me that no one at the USO admitted knowing anything about her torch. To ease my conscience, I sent her money to replace it if she could.

Margaret wrote me so often that six or seven letters would sometimes "catch up" with me at one time. Without denying my obvious charm, I feel obliged to mention that marrying an American soldier, and thus becoming a United States citizen, was the objective of many English girls. However, I do not question Margaret's sincerity, for her letters were very friendly, entertaining and obviously intended to boost my morale. Also, she wrote to me even after she married an army M.P.

29
This Is It

We were at Camp D-6 about three weeks, then were transported to Weymouth, where we boarded an LST to cross the English Channel. This should have taken a few hours but turbulent weather prevented our approaching the beaches for landing, so we were on that bouncing flat-bottom boat for three days. There were no bunks, so we slept on the wet steel deck. For meals we went from one side of the deck to the other through a small galley. When we emerged, the furious wind would blow the coffee from our cups and the food from our mess kits if we did not shield them with our hands and bodies. Many of the men were terribly seasick. I was to some extent, but never missed a meal.

We landed at LeHavre November 8. The dock and town were almost flattened by the bombing and shelling that had taken place all along the French coast. We saw very little of it, however, because it was almost nightfall when we landed, and we went directly from the loading ramp to our vehicles for a two-day "motor march." Darkness and a thick fog made visibility almost zero. Also, we drove with blackout lights, which were about as illuminating as lightning bugs. Every few minutes the roar of an aircraft passed over us in the shrouded night, sounding as if it were only a few feet high. We wondered how they could be flying so low, or flying at all in such weather. Then we learned they were "Buzz Bombs," the V-1 Rockets we had heard so much about, and we were in "Buzz Bomb Alley," the direct route from Germany to London.

The weather was cold and wet. After a few hours the welcome news spread along the column that we would stop for a coffee break. The instant we stopped, we jumped from our trucks and rushed to the chow truck with our canteen cups ready. I was among the first to have our cups filled from the twenty-gallon pot. Cold and miserable, we sipped the hot liquid eagerly. Then spewed it from our mouths amid a chorus of profanity. In the darkness, the mess sergeant had not discovered a bar of GI soap in the pot used to make the coffee. The mess sergeant escaped with his life, but if we had run across a regiment of Germans that night, our one battery could have wiped them out.

The details of the next few days—or even the next few months—have merged together, so I can only relate specific incidents, which may not be chronologically correct* Our motor march ended at a staging area near Aubel, Belgium. My gun, Gun #1, Battery B, was the first in our battalion to go on the line. For some reason, I accompanied a lieutenant and the first sergeant on a reconnaissance to locate the best terrain to "lay the battery." When we found the proper site, the lieutenant returned to the staging area to lead the battery back to our position. He left the sergeant and me at the site. We were there several hours, and had not eaten since breakfast.

---

*We had orders not to keep journals but I had a 2½ × 4½ note pad in which I made very brief, cryptic notations. This has helped me make this an accurate account.

We got so hungry that we dug up and ate some onions from the remnants of a garden.

When my gun crew arrived I rejoined them and we dug in our gun. This procedure consisted of digging out an area roughly twenty feet round and two feet deep, piling the dirt toward the front to make a barricade. Then the whole thing was covered with a camouflage net to prevent location by enemy aircraft. The net was supported, like a tent, with a number of poles. We didn't have time to dig individual slit trenches (foxholes) so we all bedded down under the net.

About two or three in the morning, I awoke with an uncomfortable sense of confinement. Under the weight of the snow that had fallen during the night, the net was sagging down within a few inches of my sleeping bag. Others were stirring, cursing and grumbling, and sleepily trying to locate a safe place to sleep. I moved my bag under one of the gun trails and tried to go back to sleep. But by now everyone was awake and Sergeant Cannady was yelling for everybody to get out and start shoveling snow off the net. The temperature had dropped sharply. We were cold all over, but particularly our feet and our hands, which were like lifeless lumps after a few minutes of raking the snow.

We worked for hours with little success. Because the snow slid down where the net had sagged, it was literally impossible for us to lift enough to slide it off the edges. Not everyone tried. I vividly remember peeping into the space around one pole seeing one man calmly eating C-rations from a can as the rest of us struggled. It was the middle of the next morning before we got all the snow off and took down the net.

This incident was our first indication that we had come into this area totally unprepared for the snow and cold. The camouflage net was made for use in the tropics and was too closely woven to let the snow go through. We had no rubber overshoes, and the water from the snow soaked through our shoes as if they were cloth. We had no field stoves or heating devices of any sort. Our training had taught us the value of conserving water and taking salt tablets to avoid heat exhaustion, but that was of little value in zero temperatures. It was weeks before we all got overshoes. Some were available, but only in small sizes. I remember borrowing overshoes which were too small and wearing them over my socks like regular shoes when I stood guard.

I will describe other "hardships" that we endured, but I feel somewhat petty in doing so because our hardships were minimal compared to those endured by the foot soldiers. I've never ceased being thankful that I was transferred into an artillery battalion before being sent overseas.

The 99th relieved the 9th Division on a twenty-two mile front along the Belgium/German border in a section of the Ardennes forest. We were stretched quite thin, but this was a "quiet" area with little activity expected. For the first few weeks our fire missions consisted mainly of harassing fire with only occasional support fire for infantry troops. We heard enemy artillery in the distance, but seldom heard the whine or the explosions of "incoming mail." Buzz bombs, at a very low altitude, passed over frequently and we could see the tracers from our anti-aircraft guns trying with infrequent success to bring them down. A greater danger to us was the occasional defective bomb that sputtered along losing altitude as it came in our direction. Fortunately, none ever landed in our immediate area.

One bit of excitement came during a fire mission

when the gunner pulled the lanyard and, instead of the usual jarring blast, there was a fizzling "pop." The projectile flew weakly from the barrel and hit the ground about ten feet away. The crew scrambled wildly for their foxholes, but the projectile did not explode. As a safety feature in explosive shells the fuse will not set off the explosive until a powder train is created by the spin of the projectile in transit. In this instance, the projectile had not traveled far enough for this to occur. The powder that propels the projectile is in cloth bags and the number of bags varies depending on the distance to the target and the trajectory desired. The cartridge and the projectile come apart so the proper number of bags can be placed in the cartridge as ordered. Apparently, in this incident some bags of power had become wet. This served to teach us to "keep our powder dry" amid the snow and rain.

We changed our position only a few times, usually staying in one place long enough to prepare reasonably comfortable slit trenches for sleeping. Sometimes we found hay or straw to line them with, and sometimes covered them with logs and earth, leaving only a hole at one end to slide in. Once I even constructed a fireplace. I dug a small trench off one side for about six feet. At the outside end I made a smokestack using an ammunition box with the ends knocked out. Then I covered the open trench with shell casings and dirt. A small fire in the end that opened into my slit trench kept me warm and cozy. The length of the "flue" killed any sparks. We stood guard in two-hour shifts through the night and when it was my turn I left a little fire burning in my fireplace and stood with my overcoat draped over the ammunition box. Another luxury I enjoyed was the delicious aroma of a chocolate bar from a K ration in the warmth of my trench.

Several times five or six of us dug a community shelter long enough to sleep toe-to-toe and wide enough for three sleeping bags. It was deep enough that we could sit up on ammunition boxes and we spent many hours doing so, playing poker by the light of a burning rag in a bottle of gasoline. The heavy smoke saturated our hair and clothing and turned our faces sooty black. Since we seldom shaved and never bathed, it's possible we would not have been considered socially acceptable in some circles.

Also, most of our conversations, replete with profanity, vulgarity and X-rated subject-matter, would not have been acceptable. I didn't contribute to most such conversations; not because of any moral superiority, but simply because I didn't speak the language. If I had been fluent in Cursing I would have been a sergeant by the time I left Fort Sill.

Despite their macho, ribald way of talking, I know that most of the men felt homesick and lonely much of the time. There is no more melancholy feeling than that of being isolated from all humanity by the confines of a foxhole, and not knowing when if ever you will be back home. I know it doesn't evoke an image of a heroic soldier on the field of battle, but I confess at such times I often looked long and longingly at my billfold souvenirs of my Secret Love. The words on the back of her photo became so impressed on my mind that I would recognize the handwriting even now. I studied with anguished yearning her picture and the scarlet imprint of her lips. I wondered if she ever thought of me or intimate moments we had shared.

30
Battle of the Bulge

December 16, 1944, our life of leisure came to an abrupt end. I was on guard duty when, at 5:30 A.M., the sky toward the east lit up in a great semi-circle and a thunderous roar of explosions shook the air. As startled soldiers emerged from their holes the field phone rang and yells of "Fire mission! Battery adjust!" mingled with the roar.

Our guns began barking their reply to the German dogs of war. Without pause, we fired as fast as we could and it was quite alarming to see the elevation of the gun barrel steadily decreasing as our targets came closer. After a few hours we were in danger of hitting the dirt parapet in front of the gun, so we pulled it from the dugout and began firing from higher ground. By then the Germans had driven so far forward on our right flank that we were firing practically at a right angle to the original front. And we were running out of shells. Ammunition trucks could not get through to replenish our supply, so by early afternoon we had nothing left but smoke shells, which had no destructive power. Completely impotent and in danger of being surrounded, we welcomed the "March Order" when it came down. Our driver, Clarence "Columbus" Cumberledge, arrived with our truck. We hastily loaded our gear, hitched the gun, and got underway.

I believe I remember correctly that all the guns of the

Battalion got out okay except for three guns in Battery C, which had to be abandoned when guns and trucks were stuck in mud. I don't think any men were killed, but several in the Signal Section were captured. As our convoy sped westward on the one road out of the area the Germans began shelling us. Lying atop the barracks bags, shells, picks, shovels and other equipment on the truck, we felt helpless and vulnerable as the shells exploded before and behind us, first on one side of the road then the other as the enemy "bracketed us in." I visualized what would happen when—not *if*—a shell struck us and wondered if the ammunition we carried, even though only smoke shells, would explode and add to the carnage. Then suddenly, perhaps because they found a more threatening target, the shelling ceased.

After about an hour of driving, we stopped. We had no ammunition but we "laid" the battery in firing position so we would be ready if ammunition arrived. However, we were not ordered to dig in the guns. We were grateful for this as we had been working strenuously since 5:30 that morning and had eaten nothing since mid-afternoon the day before. The fresh memory of the shelling of our convoy compelled us to dig protective slit trenches in the frozen ground but I was so exhausted that I dug only about eighteen inches deep and barely two feet wide. Intending to cover the trench, I found a limb that had been blown off a nearby tree but, even though it was not very large, I was amazed to find I was too weak to drag it. I had heard of foot soldiers continuing to fight after three or four days without food. This made it seem impossible. We were ravenous when we finally went to our mess truck for food just before dark.

The ground was covered with several inches of snow, it was very cold and the temperature continued to drop during the night. Icicles formed on the sides of my slit trench and because it was so narrow it was like sleeping in an icebox. I lay there trying to go to sleep, thinking I would finally get warm in my sleeping bag, but to no avail. My teeth chattered and I literally shook all over. I've heard that it is dangerous to go to sleep when suffering from hypothermia, so possibly the soldier on guard duty saved my life when he summoned me to pull my two-hour tour in the middle of the night. Walking back and forth and jumping up and down, I finally stopped my shivering and chattering teeth.

About an hour into my guard duty, around one o'clock in the morning the field phone rang. The officer calling was obviously scared to death. Breathing hard and talking with difficulty he said, "March order! We're almost surrounded and we're pulling out. This is not a withdrawal, it's a retreat!"

I thought that didn't sound very heroic, but I ran from foxhole to foxhole, shaking the men and yelling pretty much the same words. I was excited, perhaps even frightened, but not unduly so. My main concern was that some of the men might be so sluggish and exhausted that they would go back to sleep and be left behind.

The next few hours were hectic. I only knew what was happening in my field of vision, but apparently the Germans kept cutting off our escape route or there were differences of opinion as to the way out. A note in my cryptic journal reads, "Turned round. T.R. T.R., etc." and I remember reversing our direction several times before we finally made our way through the Ardennes forest on a logging trail. By then we were sleeping fitfully, sprawled atop the loaded truck. Then our slow progress came to a halt. The heavy traffic had churned the snow and soil together into a sticky mush and we were stuck. Sergeant

Cannady, who rode in the cab with the driver, jumped out and yelled for us to get down and push. Frank Winfrey, an illiterate hillbilly from Kentucky, strong as an ox and a good man, jumped down immediately, as did I. If I remember correctly, the other six men, cold, miserable and sleepy, lay like lumps and never moved. The sticky mud came halfway to our knees, but with the three of us pushing and with Cumberledge skillfully operating the clutch, we got the truck free and started forward again.

Early in the morning we arrived at a Quartermaster kitchen that had been set up in what I believe was a picnic area in a wooded region on the side of a hill. As we ate breakfast on the picnic tables we watched foot soldiers from the Second Division marching by on their way to the front. They knew we were "green" troops who had just fled from the area toward which they were moving so, perhaps to impress us, they marched with a macho, taunting bravado. We were appropriately humiliated but we were also relieved to see these seasoned reinforcements.

Before going back to battle positions we rendezvoused in a large flat area while, I suppose, the powers that be were figuring out what to do. We were there for hours and I remember feeling extremely vulnerable and wondering why we were there, like sitting ducks, waiting for enemy artillery to zero in. Above the rumble of distant explosions, which had not ceased since the German attack began, I heard a strange metallic clanking sound and the muffled roar of engines. A cloud of smoke arose in the distance and then a column of German tanks came into view on a roadway at the foot of a distant hill. We had just heard the news about the Malmedy Massacre, in which the Germans gathered almost 100 American prisoners in a field and opened fire with machine guns, killing almost all. Now, seeing these ominous, monstrous tanks lumbering in our direction, I had the most acute feeling of peril since the war began.

I felt a tremendous sense of relief when we pulled out and went on line. By then we had ammunition again and were firing regularly. The constant fog that had been with us for weeks had dispersed enough for air activity and one day German bombers concentrated on our site. I was on duty at the gun (we normally had four men on duty and four off) when the bombing began. Looking up, we saw a bomb released directly overhead, but instead of spiraling down in the usual way it was tumbling end over end. Apparently this slowed its fall, or perhaps it was the same phenomenon that had made me feel as if I were moving in slow motion when I was thrown from the overturning truck in Texas. In any case, it seemed as though the bomb was falling ever so slowly toward us. As it loomed near, we scrambled for our foxholes. The bomb hit on the left side of our gun, knocking dirt on us as we ran, but instead of exploding it bounced over our gun and came to rest about twenty feet on the other side. We knew about delayed fuses, so we dived into our trenches.

Our mail clerk happened to be in our vicinity and, of course, he had no trench of his own. He dived into mine, where I was lying face up. I had been praying devoutly, and I thanked God for sending this extra protection. Even so, I felt a little uncomfortable with our intimate position. Fortunately he was considerably shorter than I and we were toe to toe rather than face to face. We lay there for what seemed an eternity, but was probably only a minute or so, then got up and ran as hard as we could to put more distance between us and the bomb. We kept that distance until the bomb squad arrived hours later to defuse it.

I had been appointed an "official" reporter for the

Stars and Stripes* and sent in the story of the dud bomb. It was published along with a cartoon showing the bomb bouncing over our gun.

I believe we made one more withdrawal before the American defense solidified and we dug in at Elsenborn Ridge, which was the termination point for the German "bulge."

Thanks to the determination of the commanding generals, we, and I understand the infantry as well, had turkey and dressing in our mess kits Christmas Day. It seems to me that Christmas was rather quiet, but activity resumed the following day. We had fire missions at frequent intervals, but four men were normally off duty, which gave us time to enhance our "living quarters." Five of us on Gun #1 dug and covered a community foxhole, which we occupied for about two weeks. One thing I remember particularly well about the location is the route to the mess truck, about three hundred yards to our rear. The path led across a valley which, when we ate breakfast about ten o'clock in the morning, was like a river of fog. It was so dense that when we walked down into it we disappeared until we emerged on the other side. Then we turned right to reach our chow truck, which was parked near the end of a huge concrete parapet that had been the target range when this area was a German army camp.

Our mess section had "liberated" a large supply of German buckwheat, ersatz butter and thick syrup, similar to the sorghum syrup from my childhood at the Old Home Place. For about two weeks our morning meal consisted of this syrup, butter and buckwheat pancakes

---

*The Army's official newspaper since the Civil War.

served with boiling hot coffee. Because the weather was so cold, this breakfast of hot pancakes and coffee was the highlight of the day. We would squat to eat, setting our mess cups in the snow to cool because, otherwise, the metal could literally burn blisters on our lips. With scientific precision I discovered the coffee was the right temperature when one-half the cup was melted into the snow. Since there was an ample supply, we could go back for more pancakes as many times as desired. Some men ate unbelievable amounts. On the morning of December 28 Pfc. Empfield set a record by eating, if I remember correctly, twelve pancakes. The guys kidded him about it and I suspect everybody in the Battery heard about this feat.

In the afternoon of December 28 we were playing poker in the Gun #1 "condominium." Our medic, who we called "Pop" Metz because of his advanced age (he was almost thirty) was playing with us. We were so accustomed to the sound of explosions that we didn't notice when an incoming shell exploded only fifty feet or so away near the dugout next to ours. Someone stuck his head inside our entrance and yelled excitedly that they had been hit and needed the medic fast. Pop rushed to their dugout but Empfield, who had been hit in the chest, was dead by the time he arrived.

Beginning the day after Christmas there was increasing air activity as the weather cleared. It was about this time that we saw our first German jets. It was like watching an old Buck Rogers movie* seeing those planes without propellers zipping through the air. Even when

*Science fiction films of the late 1930s.

they were strafing in our area we stood outside our foxholes and watched in fascination, diving for cover only when they headed in our direction. Anti-aircraft guns all around started their chattering any time a plane came into view, occasionally bringing one down in flames. On New Year's Day we saw a tremendous "dogfight" between the German planes and ours. We saw planes on both sides go down. One of our pilots was particularly tenacious, escaping from the quick German craft then returning to the fray time after time. We watched with admiration, and we groaned in horror when his plane burst into flames. His chute opened and we prayed as if he were a close friend that he landed safely.

Thanks to the heroic determination of the infantry, aided by the artillery and air force, the Germans began to fall back and the Battle of the Bulge melded into the Remagen Bridgehead and the Battle of the Ruhr Pocket.

31
Scenes of War

We moved with increasing frequency, seldom staying more than a day or so in the same spot. Fire missions were frequent as we were called on to support infantry wiping out pockets of resistance. Each Battery had a forward observer with a radio to call for artillery as needed. His requests, and those from superior Command Posts, were relayed to the Battery CP, from which telephone wires ran to the guns. When the field phone rang the gun crew sergeant, or someone in his place, answered and relayed the commands to the crew. For example: "Fire mission! Battery adjust. Shell HE* Fuse quick. Charge five. SI** 10. Elevation 100. Base deflection Right 15. Fire when ready."

The sequence of the commands was such that different crewmen completed their specific tasks at approximately the same time. By the time the projectile was rammed into the gun the "Number 1 Man" would be ready to close the breech block and have the barrel raised to the proper elevation. The gunner would have set the panoramic sight and traversed the barrel so the aiming stakes lined up in the sight. Number One would call, "Set," the gunner, "Ready," and the sergeant, "Fire!"

*Heavy explosive.
**Site inclination.

On one occasion I missed the opportunity to become a "hero," sort of. I was off duty sitting twenty-five feet or so behind the gun, reading and halfway watching the gun crew at work. I was startled to see the "Number 1 man" furiously cranking, decreasing the elevation of the gun an abnormal amount. I *almost* yelled, "Cease fire!" but on second thought decided they were simply flattening the trajectory by increasing the charge. That turned out to be true, but the "Number 4 man" had missed the unusual command to change the charge in the middle of a mission and had not added the extra bag of powder. After a few seconds the sergeant yelled, "Cease fire," and there was consternation among the crew. The round had fallen among our own infantry. No one was hurt; but even though he did nothing wrong the officer giving the command, Lt. Tom Porter, took full responsibility. As punishment, according to rumor among the enlisted men, he was transferred to the front as a forward observer.

Occasionally we were given information as to the nature of our target. Once Lt. Porter, who was highly respected by us all because of the considerate way he treated us, was wounded while on duty up front. He was pinned down in a foxhole, and we were called on to lay down a barrage to enable rescuers to reach him. This gave a personal purpose to our efforts, and we let out a delighted cheer when informed that he was okay.

When we started moving into the areas that had been occupied by the enemy, we saw some of the results of our bombardments: damaged tanks and trucks, dead horses* and dead Germans lying haphazardly in the

---

*The Germans still used some horse drawn artillery.

snow. We never saw American bodies, probably because our Grave Service picked them up as soon as possible. The frigid temperature was an ironic blessing in that it preserved the bodies until they could be properly identified and removed.

Perhaps the most poignant sight I remember was an old man driving a wagon slowly through the village of Remagen picking up the bodies of civilian dead. They were then piled in a hilltop cemetery near our bivouac until they could be properly buried. I had to pass this scene as I walked guard; and the sight of those men, women (some nude) and children, haphazardly heaped on each other almost made me ill.

One of the notes in my abbreviated journal reads, "Rem. dead Jerry by war monument." Strangely, I cannot remember this scene, which apparently impressed me with its irony. I do remember seeing a young German soldier in a sitting position, propped against something as if he had been placed there, with his chest blown away exposing his entrails. Perhaps it was a war monument he was propped against.

As we advanced into German many displaced persons, slave laborers, were freed. Eventually these were gathered into repatriation centers, but initially some of them began walking to get out of Germany and closer to home. They encountered tremendous hardships in finding food. We not only had our army rations; but we also foraged the houses we sometimes occupied, particularly for fresh eggs and chickens. Once we stayed a day or so in a house from which the civilians had fled. Someone killed a chicken, cutting off its head and throwing it into the backyard. Later I was looking out from a second floor window and saw an Indian (from India) walking across the yard. He picked up the chicken head and gnawed at it hungrily. I threw him a K-ration chocolate bar. Instead of devouring it as I expected, he furtively tucked it into his pocket and hurried away.

There were many other pitiful scenes, but I have related only enough to attest to the horrors of war. Thankfully, there were other scenes and events less grim, some even amusing.

32
Baths and R & R

Among the equipment on our tow truck was a pyramidal tent, which was large enough for the complete gun crew to sleep in. We seldom had the opportunity to use it—probably only two or three times altogether. About the middle of February we were off the line for a few days so we pitched our tent on a gently sloping spot in a snow-covered field. We shoveled away just enough snow to make room for our sleeping bags on the frozen ground. In the middle of the night we felt an uncomfortable wetness and awoke to find that the snow was melting and we were lying in a rising flood. I dragged myself outside, and found that a light rain was adding volume to the water from the melting snow. I found enough empty ammo boxes to make a platform, a sort of island, to sleep on the rest of the night. Grumbling and cursing from the other men suggested they were not as resourceful.

From the time we left Elsenborn Ridge we moved so often and covered so many miles that I cannot remember much in sequence, but only a few unusual events. Such as taking a bath. Once I became so uncomfortably filthy that I walked back to our motor pool, found my barracks bag on our truck and dug out a clean pair of long underwear. Even though the temperature was around freezing, I stripped and bathed with water in my helmet before donning the clean underclothes.

On another occasion, we were temporarily in a rest area and Quartermaster brought in a shower unit—a truck with a hot water tank and a shower. We lined up naked in a field, were herded through the shower and then given clean underwear, pants and shirts.

Once our officers set up their command post in a house, which had a big kitchen with a wood-burning stove and also a portable tin bathtub. Some of us enlisted men were given the opportunity to bathe while these luxurious facilities were available. It was pleasant sitting in that tub of warm water, but would have been more so if it had not been in the middle of the kitchen with officers and enlisted men sitting all around.

The only other baths I remember during a period of about five months were when I went to Verviers, Belgium, on a three-day "R & R"* pass.

On February 26 a group of us were loaded into a 2½ ton truck for a trip of forty miles or so back to Verviers, where a huge R & R camp had been set up. The first memorable event occurred when I left my duffel bag on my selected bunk in the barracks and rushed to the shower. When I returned I found someone had rifled my bag and taken all the cigarettes and K-ration chocolate bars I had brought along for bartering. It was most unlikely that I would have used them anyway, certainly not for the usual purpose, but it was a disheartening beginning to my leave.

Three other guys and I walked downtown and they insisted on stopping at a well-advertised house of ill repute. I went in with them but while they went upstairs with some of the entertainers I sat in the kitchen and

---

*Rest and recreation.

talked with the "madam." In earlier years she had been an actress in England, and she spoke English quite well. We had an engrossing conversation about her career, the war and life in general. She was cooking cabbage in an iron skillet on a wood stove, and occasionally her husband came through, bringing in wood and doing various chores. He didn't appear to be in good health and had a persistent, unhealthy-sounding cough. Whenever he coughed, she impatiently snapped, "Fermez la bouche!"*

I glanced at my watch and realized the madam and I had been talking quite a while. I went into the parlor and asked one of the ladies in my fractured French, "Ou est mes amis?"** She wasn't very friendly, perhaps because I hadn't bought anything, but she told me they left some time ago. Either they didn't know I was in the kitchen with the madam or they thought my prudence might inhibit their plans for the day. In any case, I spent the rest of the day on my own and amused myself by composing rhymes in my mind about the things I saw as I walked around. For example:

Four times I saw a pair of girls,
Parting, tell each other "Au revoir."
Each kissed the other fondly on the cheek,
Once on each, or twice, or even more.

Displeased, I shook my head from side to side,
And gazed contemptuous on the parting misses.
What a sacrilegious act I had espied,
What a sinful waste of kisses!

*Shut your mouth!"
**Where *is* my friends?"

And, when I walked into a huge Catholic cathedral:

The oaken doors, gigantic, heavy, tall,
Make him who enters feel exceeding small.
But inside the silent church God seems so near and real
One stands in humble awe and feels—smaller still.

33
I Make Corporal; Germans Surrender!

The commanding officer of Battery B was Captain Frois. He was not a large man, but wiry and tough, a "man's man" who led by example. He truly would not ask us to do anything he wouldn't do. I respected him very much and I had the feeling that it was a mutual respect. However, there were a number of incidents that might call into question the reasonableness of my thinking so. On one occasion he called me on the carpet—actually the dirt floor of his dugout—when he censored one of my letters and detected a rather transparent attempt to tell my family we were serving with the First Army. This would have enabled them to tell where we were and what was happening to our unit by listening to the daily news. Knowing that the enemy already knew full well what units made up the First Army, I said, a bit flippantly, that I would be more subtle next time. He informed me sternly that there better not be a next time.

Once I happened to be at the CP and Captain Frois asked me to deliver a Jeep to the motor pool. When I told him I couldn't drive, he looked at me in disbelief and said, "Didn't they have cars in Georgia?"

I said, "Yes, but we didn't own it."

However, knowing I was an amateur magician, once during a boring interval he summoned me to the CP to do card tricks for the officers and seemed quite impressed. Also, one time he had me do a series of orientation classes to bring the men up to date on the progress of the war, and he appointed me as the battery's official reporter for the *Stars and Stripes.*

Sometime in March, I was promoted to Corporal and assigned as a Scout, a part of the forward observer team. I was then often close enough to see individual soldiers in the enemy's front lines. But by then we had crossed into Germany and were moving forward sometimes forty miles in a day, so my experience up front with the foot soldiers was very limited.

I shared with another corporal the duty of carrying the radio. This was a bulky, heavy instrument mounted on a board with straps to carry it like a backpack. During one of the first days I was up front with the infantry we moved into Aachen, a border town that was mostly a pile of rubble because of all the fighting that had taken place there. As I was standing beside the street with the radio on my back, a weary-looking column of infantrymen plodded by. It was Company G of the 393rd Regiment, the company I had trained with before being transferred to the 371st. One particularly rough-looking soldier, who could have been the model for a Bill Mauldin* cartoon, caught my eye. He was the intellectual, classical-music-loving man who was my "buddy" at Camp Maxey. I fell in beside him and asked how he'd been doing. He let me know with a string of profanity that left no doubt.

Perhaps this is the proper place to mention that 450

---

*Famed cartoonist who expressed the essence of the war with humor and pathos, capturing the hearts of soldiers and civilians as well.

men, one in six of the 393rd Infantry Regiment, were killed during and following the Battle of the Bulge. Twelve men, one in 33 of the 271st were killed during the same time.*

Somewhere I had liberated a full-size office typewriter, which was just like an American machine except for a few extra letters. I kept it in my barracks bag on my crew's 2½ ton truck except when there was an opportune time to use it. Because I seldom had a table or chair, I typed sitting on the floor with the typewriter sitting on the floor between my legs, putting my hands under my knees to reach the keyboard. One day toward the end of April the Battery CP was set up in a house and I was in an upstairs room, sitting on the floor, typing. Someone yelled, "Stanfield, report to Captain Frois on the double."

I decided to do so.

Downstairs, the captain said, "Stanfield, how would you like to get a field commission?"

I was totally shocked. One of our enlisted men, Joe McNulty, had been given a field commission, but that was for bravery and service beyond the call of duty. Nothing I had done came close to reaching that plateau. I managed to reply, "I'd like it very much, sir."

"Well, we need an Air Observer. You'll have to be able to fly in an emergency, so we're arranging lessons for you. You'll be commissioned as soon as you qualify."

Based on my past experience—being assigned to the Air Corps and ending up in the Infantry—I knew I was a long way from the cockpit of an airplane, but I was walking on air. Judiciously, I did not write or talk to anyone

---

*Approximate figures. Ratios for wounded and captured probably about the same.

about this remarkable turn of events. But in my mind I went over the lyrics to *Mairzy Doats* to be sure I still remembered them.

On April 30 Adolf Hitler committed suicide, and May 2 the war in Europe was over. It was a tremendously joyful occasion, and I am ashamed to admit just a trace of chagrin that my chance of getting a commission was also over.

Early on the morning of June 15, those of us with insufficient "points" for discharge left by motor convoy to join the 2nd Division in Czechoslovakia. I still remember the melancholy atmosphere and the sad expression on Captain Frois* face as he watched us depart.

We reached our destination late that day and bivouacked in a hillside cherry orchard. I have a photo of Sergeant Cannady taking a bath in a tin tub on that hillside, which is the last location where we were together. Some of us paid some Czech ladies to remove the 99th Checkerboard Insignia from our uniforms and sew on the 2nd Division patch. After being informed that we would be going home for thirty-day furloughs, then to the Pacific, we made a four-day motor march to Reims, France. There we were quartered in a huge "tent city," called Camp Norfolk, while arrangements were made for transportation to the States.

We had folding cots and were quite comfortable, ten to a tent. It was balmy weather and we would roll up the sides of the tents and move the cots outside for sunbathing. After a few relaxing days, however, we were told to shave and shape up. The usual routine of reveille, calis-

---

*Captain Frois remained in the army, became a colonel and was killed in the Korean war.

thenics, close-order drill, evening retreat and taps began. However, a special effort was made to give every man a 24-hour pass so that he could visit Paris. With diabolical efficiency, the Army had made sure that no two friends were transferred to the same unit, but I had become friendly with one guy, an original 2nd Division man, and we arranged to go on pass at the same time. Trucks left early one morning for the three-hour drive and dropped us off at a bridge over the Seine River in the middle of Paris. We were warned that the trucks would meet us there and leave for the return trip precisely at midnight.

Along with most of the others, my friend and I made a bee line for "Pig Alley,"* known for its risqué entertainment and plenteous prostitutes. While we were having a beer, probably about my third since joining the army, at one of the bars, a very friendly young lady came up to us and sweetly asked, "Zigzig?" I thought she was asking for a cigarette, but learned better when my friend accompanied her to an upstairs apartment. Lest it appear that I was not "normal" I confess to being sorely tempted. I know that "conscience gets a lot of credit that belongs to cold feet," but in any event I did not enter into any contract for services. I waited uncomfortably until my friend returned, and then suggested we walk around to see some of the sights of the city. He was more interested in his beer and Pig Alley, so we decided to split up. I saw the Eiffel Tower, Arc de Triomphe, Cathedral de Notre Dame and the outside only of the Louvre. I must have eaten, but can't remember where or what. Well before midnight I was waiting at the bridge and my friend, a little

*Pigalle, a section of Paris.

bleary-eyed and disheveled, was also there in time to board the truck back to Camp Norfolk.

July 12 we boarded ship in LeHavre bound for New York. There is a strange gap in my memory regarding that voyage, but I remember the sight of the Statue of Liberty and a sense of relief when we set foot on American soil. However, after several aborted chances to become an Officer and a Gentleman, I was returning as a mere corporal with only the prospect of serving as a replacement, a "beginner" again, in the gruesome warfare with the Japanese. I had no real sense of pride, and I had no sweetheart waiting to welcome me home. Haunting memories of my Secret Love added to my despondent mood.

34
Back in the States

We landed in New York July 20, 1945, were sorted out and put on troop trains to various points across the country. My train arrived at Ft. MacPherson about July 25. The railroad track into the fort ran behind the post office, where Rebecca and her friend Louise Carroll were working at that time. It was a beautiful sight when I saw them standing outside the back door watching as the troop train rolled slowly by. My thirty-day furlough began as soon as the checking-in process was completed.

At that time Rebecca and Margaret were boarding with a Mrs. Akers in College Park, south of East Point. The rest of the family had moved to Macon, where Daddy and Freeman had been working for the creosote plant since 1941, and were living in a basement apartment on Vineville Avenue. I can't remember, but assume that I rode a Greyhound bus from Atlanta to Macon, perhaps after first visiting with Rebecca and Margaret. None of my family was very demonstrative, so there were no emotional hugs and kisses, but it was a happy reunion both in Atlanta and Macon.

I had no friends in Macon and I believe the only person besides my sisters that I saw in Atlanta was Hazel Watts. We had corresponded while I was overseas and had a friendship that was somewhere between passionate and Platonic, definitely closer to the latter. So I decided to use part of my furlough to go visit my relatives in Tennessee. Uncle Will had died of cancer, but I visited Aunt Lydia and Aunt Betty and Uncle Tom Forrest. I think I spent just one night in Waverly, then caught the bus for home.

I had a two-hour layover in Nashville. About the time our bus arrived on August 15, the streets filled with people, laughing and yelling, hugging and kissing in jubilant joy. Japan had surrendered! The war was over! I stood in the street in front of the bus station, feeling somewhat alone among the crowd and apparently looking very dejected. A young girl came up, said, "You look like you need a kiss," and proceeded to hug and kiss me.

The only two people I knew who lived in Nashville were the McNeil twins, Jean and Jo. Amazingly, as I stood in the jostling throng I saw Jo on the corner looking somewhat agitated. She was tremendously surprised when I grabbed her arm. She had been trying to catch a streetcar but they were all stalled in the crush of cars and people. She was trying to get to a dance at a high school several miles away.

I found a cab and the driver managed to thread his way through the crowded streets to the school. Jean was already at the school gym and I said I would like to go in to see her. Jo said, "Of course. I know she'd like to see you."

But I sensed she was not overly exuberant about my intrusion. I had the driver wait for me while I went in. The cluttering, laughing kids seemed much younger than I. Jean greeted me with surprise and friendliness, but the warmth and camaraderie that we felt when we visited at Uncle Will's house three years before were no longer there. I said goodbye and had the cab take me back to the bus station. That was the last contact I ever had with Jean and Jo.

In Macon, knowing now that I would be discharged shortly, I went to Mercer University and applied for enrollment under the "GI Bill." They received my transcript from the University of Arkansas, credited me with the hours earned there, and approved my enrollment to begin the next semester, December 10.

I visited Atlanta at least once more before my furlough ended and my Secret Love was constantly on my mind while I was there. As I had done hundreds of times before, I tried to determine in a logical way what her actual feelings had been toward me. Perhaps it was wishful thinking, but I concluded she actually did love me. It was not logical that she was simply "playing" with me to occupy her time. Certainly she could have found someone who would have provided her with better transportation than streetcars, better food than Krystal hamburgers and more exciting entertainment than movies and walking the streets of Atlanta. Once I was drafted, it wasn't logical that she would have ridden streetcars to visit me and sat on park benches in the cold night if she had not cared for me.

I finally got up the nerve to call the company where she had worked and talked with a girl who had known her. I found that she had, indeed, married her fiancé but shortly afterward had become ill with a fast-acting cancer and died before her twenty-first birthday. She had been alive to me only in my memory for almost three years, so there was not the overflowing grief that normally comes with news that a loved one has died. But it welled up within, and stayed there for many years. Our brief romance had been secret, just between us. And so my grief was secret, too.

When my furlough ended August 25, 1945, I rejoined the Second Division, 37th Field Artillery in Camp Swift, Texas. I was assigned to Headquarters doing clerical work and, about a month later transferred to McCloskey General Hospital, Temple, Texas, for similar work there. My principal duty at the hospital was checking records to be sure all the patients had been awarded the medals to which they were entitled. That was a lot of medals. The hospital was filled with men who had lost an arm or a leg or had been otherwise seriously injured.

I was discharged November 29, 1945. I was twenty-two years old.

So ended the days of my youth.

35
Macon, after the War

After my discharge from the army, I went by train to Atlanta and from there by bus to Macon. My family had moved from their basement apartment to a nice house on Buckingham Place, still close enough to the creosote plant for Daddy and Freeman to walk to work; Daddy would not have had it any other way. It was only a few steps from the nearest bus stop and within two miles of Mercer University, where I began classes December 10.

The G.I. Bill paid my tuition and $50.00 per month for subsistence. After a few weeks I realized the $50.00 per month was not sufficient, so I got a job at Matthews Dairy, a combination dairy/ice cream store about halfway between Buckingham Place and Mercer. I walked to work when I got out of school and dipped ice cream and made milk shakes until we closed at 9:00 or 10:00 P.M., depending on the season. I also worked most weekends, but there were times during the day when I could study while on the job. Earlier I mentioned that my family was not very demonstrative. I cannot remember my mother ever hugging or kissing me. But every evening that I worked at the ice cream parlor she prepared a home-cooked supper for me and she or Freeman or one of my sisters brought it to me. I always considered that a more convincing symbol of love than a hug or a kiss.

Life was a little easier for Mother than it had been in

the past but, since Daddy and Freeman came home for lunch, she still cooked three meals a day. She did the housework, washing and ironing, for a total of seven: herself, Daddy, Freeman, Bettie, Bee, Pat and me. Bettie did stenographic work at Warner Robins Air Base, about fifteen miles south of Macon. Pat was in high school and Bee attended Wesleyan College. Rebecca, Margaret, and W.T. remained in Atlanta.

After years of hard work and faithful service, Freeman was promoted to Superintendent of the creosote plant, and as such was given the privilege of moving with his family into a company-owned house on the premises. It was not a fancy house, but quite adequate, and all utilities were furnished by the company. Also, there was a swimming pool. Actually, it had been built as a reservoir for water used in the plant operation, but had been purposely designed for use as a swimming pool as well. It was never back washed, vacuumed or chlorinated, but apparently the creosote it absorbed from the air prevented algae or other organic matter. Except for a slight oily film on top, the water appeared clear and clean. It was a welcome refuge when the muggy Macon temperature reached one hundred or more, as it frequently did. Daddy was approaching sixty years of age and had not been swimming since we left Big Richland Creek in 1935. But one hot day we talked him into donning a bathing suit—probably the only time in his life he ever wore one—to cool off in the pool. Instead of stepping gently in, he approached running and "div"* in headfirst, making a considerable splash. He swam around with his old fash-

---

*Daddy's word for "dived."

ioned breast stroke for a few minutes, and seemed to enjoy it, but that was the only time we ever got him into the pool. Pat's high school friends sometimes came by for a swim, and a couple of boys she (or Bee) had known in Atlanta came down once and went for a swim while there. Nobody died as a result of swimming in that creosote-flavored pool—as far as we know.

Shortly after we moved into the company house Uncle Tom, Daddy's older brother who had never married, came to visit. Mother was used to making room for one more and we all made Uncle Tom feel at home. He got a job with a small independent grocer and stayed. With eight people in a rather small five-room house, which was miserably hot in the summer, and with one bath, we were not exactly living in luxury. However, we had the "cement pond," we had a badminton court on the ample lawn and, overall, it was a pleasant location. Every few hours a freight train passed on the tracks about a hundred feet from the house, but we got so used to it that it didn't even awaken us at night.

Because I worked during most of my time off campus, and was not particularly gregarious anyway, I wasn't involved in many extracurricular activities and had only a few school friends. One of them was Bob Buchanan, who occasionally gave me a lift from school to my job. Bob was studying law while I was majoring in journalism, but we were together in a number of classes. He had lost a leg in the war, but it didn't slow him down. One day I mentioned that I had never ridden in an airplane. We were in his car at the time, so he headed for the Macon airfield and we paid five dollars apiece for a pilot to take us up for a fifteen-minute flight. When Bob discovered that I couldn't drive a car, he was amazed. He insisted on teaching me and, after a couple of brief lessons, pronounced me ready to get my license. That particular day the Highway Patrol was giving tests in Perry, a town just south of Macon, so Bob drove us down there in his car. I took the test and finally, at the age of twenty-three, got my first driver's license.

It happened that about this time one night at the ice cream parlor I got a surprising telephone call. It was Gretchen Stockford, the girl who had ditched me for a second lieutenant at the University of Arkansas. She had not married and was then living in Jacksonville, Florida. She invited me to drive down to see her. I would have gone—I had a driver's license and I still remembered the words to *Mairzy Doatz*—but there was the small matter of not having a car. I told her it was hard for me to get away from my job as manager of a busy ice cream parlor.

Occasionally I had a weekend off and caught a Greyhound bus to Atlanta for a date with Anne Duke, my friend from the halcyon days before the war. She had served in the WAVES and we had renewed our friendship when both of us were on furlough shortly before our discharges and ran into each other at the Greyhound bus station. We became more than "just friends," but she eventually met and married a better man. Perhaps this would not have happened except that, unknown to her, it was a sort of *Ricochet Romance*.* I still mourned my Secret Love. As a sort of catharsis for my unshared grief, I wrote a long, romanticized poem about her. That, too, was secret: I didn't let anyone else read it for forty-five years.**

---

*Name of a song popular at that time.
**The poem appears in a collection of my poetry published in 1995.
  First printing, 1 copy.

Despite the undercurrent of sadness in my life at that time, I enjoyed my studies at Mercer. Since Bee was also in college we had a lot of "intellectual" conversations about our schoolwork. At that time few in our economic status attended college. For me, it was made possible by the GI Bill, and Bee had been awarded a two-year scholarship to Wesleyan when she graduated from Russell High School in East Point. After the two years she left because of lack of funds, even though W.T. offered to pay her tuition. She was an "A" student and particularly excelled in literature and writing. After she left, the *Wesleyan Magazine* published one of her short stories with a foreword by the editor praising her talent and expressing regret that she was no longer there.

I liked to write, also, but my writing was mostly confined to school essays and entries in advertising "Jingle Contests," which were popular at that time. I remember especially one contest that was sponsored by Pepsodent Toothpaste. First prize was a "brand new car" for the best two-line jingle beginning "My Favorite Brunette*" My entry was:

My favorite brunette with all her cute wiles
Entices me most with her Pepsodent smiles.

A few days before the winner was to be announced on the Bob Hope radio show I received a registered letter with an affidavit to sign to the effect that my entry was original and that I had no relatives working for Pepsodent. I had won prizes in other contests without

---

*Title of a movie starring Bob Hope and Dorothy Lamour.

such formality, so I knew that I had won the car. I hardly slept for several nights preceding the scheduled announcement of the winner. The words to *Mairzy Doatz* began to sing in my mind as I envisioned a trip to Jacksonville and strategies to get Gretchen into the back seat of that car. The night of the announcement we gathered excitedly around the radio. I've forgotten the name announced, but I remember quite well that it wasn't mine.

I was dismally depressed for days. It was small consolation when I received the notice that I had won the second prize, a refrigerator. This, and a washing machine I won in another contest, were the first major appliances we ever owned. Among other prizes I won were a year's supply of washing detergent and a year's supply of nylon hose, which still didn't make up for not winning that car.

36
The East Point Commune

When T was discharged from the army he decided to stay in Atlanta. He went to work on the assembly line for Fisher Body Works and boarded nearby with a lady who was a relative of Mr. Bogus—the man who owned the Clydeton General Store when we lived at Harris Hooper's Place twenty years earlier. Mother had known this lady for many years and often talked with her on the telephone. I don't know if she put W.T. in touch with her or if he found her by coincidence while looking for a place near his work.

After a few months, T bought a jeep in a surplus property sale at Conley Army Depot and no longer needed to live within walking distance of his job. Rebecca and Margaret were still boarding with Mrs. Akers in College Park, so it would benefit them all if he and Rebecca and Margaret could live together in one place. T began looking for such a place and discovered a house for sale on Maple Street in East Point, around the corner from where we had lived on Connally Drive. It was the house where Loretta Starr had lived, across the street from the vacant lot where I began and ended my football career.

Since we were kids, mother had constantly preached to us that if we would "stick together" we could "make something of ourselves." The affect of that is reflected in a letter I wrote to Rebecca from Camp Maxey July 3, 1944.

It read in part: *"Hope you'll both invest in war bonds. There are enough of us that we should be able to pool our savings after the war and live in real comfort. We can get a lot of the modern conveniences we've done without . . . a refrigerator, good water system, nice rugs, phonograph, washing machine . . . and a lot of such things."*

The girls, T and I bought war bonds regularly and turned them over to Daddy for safekeeping. Daddy, having very limited schooling, had done very little writing. He had written me one five-line letter while I was in the army, and whenever he signed his name he wrote quite slowly and always said jokingly, "Great pensman!" But he meticulously wrote the serial number of each war bond under our names on a sheet of paper that he kept folded in his wallet. We all agreed to use our bonds and other savings to make the down payment on the Maple Street house. We bought it under Daddy's name, but Mother recorded in a ledger the amount that each of us paid and later provided in her will for the refund of those amounts.

T drove the jeep to Macon one weekend to pick up whatever furniture Mother could spare. As he drove into town, he noticed a flatbed eight-foot trailer in a driveway a few blocks from our house. He did not know the people who lived there but he impulsively knocked on their door and asked them if he could borrow their trailer to move some furniture to Atlanta. If it had been anyone but T, they probably would have slammed the door in his face. But T had such an open, honest air about him that perfect strangers often treated him like an old friend. They loaned him the trailer.

The jeep and trailer loaded eight feet high could have been the model for *The Beverly Hillbillies* moving from Arkansas in the TV show twenty years later. I went with T to East Point but stayed only long enough to help move the furniture into our new house, then went back to Macon. Uncle Tom moved to East Point a few days later and I followed as soon as I finished school. Thanks to the accelerated courses I had taken at the University of Arkansas while in the army, I was able to complete the requirements for my B.A. degree in a little over two years, in March 1948. Although I was not present for the ceremony, I was graduated *Magna Cum Laude* in June that year.

Shortly after I moved to East Point, Freeman and W.T. decided they would drive the jeep up to Tennessee on a fishing trip. T drove to Macon to get Freeman and they came back by the house in East Point on their way to Waverly. It was still winter, there was a misty rain, and it was extremely cold. The jeep didn't have a heater, which really didn't matter since it also didn't have a top or sides. The only windshield wiper was on the driver's side. It was moved back and forth by hand with a lever on the inside of the glass. I felt so sorry for them facing a miserable eight-hour drive that I insisted that we fasten some cardboard from the windshield back along each side of the front seat. It didn't do much good. They nearly froze before they reached Waverly. However, the weather cleared and warmed up after they got there and they had a great time visiting relatives and friends. Uncle Tom Forrest took them fishing and they caught a lot of fish. The trip back wasn't too bad, but they didn't have to buy any ice for the fish.

After the great fishing expedition T and I constructed a plywood-and-Plexiglass body to enclose the jeep. We drew a sketch, but worked out the details as we went along. The finished product, painted olive drab, was not exactly "sleek," but it kept out the wind and rain quite well. It served as the family car, which we piled into and drove to Macon almost every Friday night, returning Sunday afternoon. I also particularly remember driving that jeep about twice a week to the Atlantic Ice and Coal Company on Main Street for a fifty-pound block of ice. It fit perfectly wedged behind the front bumper.

To supplement the furniture we brought from Macon, we had bought an icebox and a gas stove which must have been among the first ever built, it was essentially an oven on legs with four open burners above. Uncle Tom, who was very capable but was what is called a "rough" carpenter, built us a dining table and a chest of drawers. He was an invaluable member of the clan, doing all sorts of repair and remodeling on the house and also changing a huge backyard from a jungle of weeds and bushes into an attractive, productive orchard and garden.

We called the Maple Street house our "commune." Almost from the start Frances Thornhill, a friend of Margaret and Rebecca, lived there with us and became like another sister. When Bee left Wesleyan in September 1947, she got a job with Alcoa Aluminum Company in Atlanta and joined us in East Point, making a total of seven. The tasks of day-to-day living were shared with practically no discord or disputes. T and I helped Uncle Tom with the maintenance and remodeling. For example, we installed electric wall receptacles, and wall switches and ceiling fixtures to replace the single light bulbs with pull switches that hung in the center of each room. We installed wallboard over clapboard in rooms that had been made by "boxing in" a back porch and, with a rented floor sander, we refinished the floors in all ten rooms of that old house.

The girls did the cooking and housekeeping. We did most of our grocery shopping once a week, sometimes three or four of us piling into the jeep and driving to Durham's grocery on Connally Drive. On one occasion T, Rebecca, Margaret and I drove to the store and when we got out T stopped to greet a man walking toward us. He shook his hand warmly, saying, "Hi, there! How you doing? Haven't seen you in years!"

The rest of us went on into the store, leaving T talking to his long-lost friend. When T came into the store we asked who he'd been talking to and he said with characteristic cheerfulness, "Oh, that was the fellow that stole my boat!"

When we individually bought groceries or other items for the household we put the receipts in a glass bowl on top of the icebox. Once a week Rebecca tallied all the receipts, collected from those who owed and reimbursed those who had overpaid their share.

Having a degree in Journalism, when I moved to East Point I applied for a job at the *Atlanta Journal*. None was available at that time, or so I was informed, so I placed an ad in the *Journal's* classified pages under "Positions Wanted." I got one response—from two men who were making documentary movies about small towns. They had no local office, so we met in the Georgian Terrace Hotel, across the street from the Fox Theater. They explained that they worked through civic clubs and chambers of commerce, emphasizing patriotism and civic pride in their films. They needed someone to write the narratives. They had worked in Hollywood before starting this venture, and had been involved in producing *The Three Stooges* films. This certainly qualified them for filming civic leaders and local politicians, so I accepted the job. I wrote one script for them, after which they went out of business. In my defense, there was ample evidence that they were *almost* out of business before I was hired.

The fact that I did not become an acclaimed Hollywood scriptwriter can be traced directly back to that fact.

I did seriously consider going to Hollywood—to attend the *Chavez College of Magic*. This was possibly the first school of magic in the country—certainly the first to be approved under the G.I. Bill. I wrote for an application and asked about the possibility of finding a job to pay my living expenses. To their credit, they answered with complete candor that it was very difficult to find a part-time job, and that they would not recommend my coming without a source of funds for subsistence. My lifelong prudence prevailed, and I continued looking for work in Atlanta.

Eventually I got three offers at the same time, another of those little pranks that fate is famous for. The most attractive offer was writing for a company that published trade magazines, but the pay was hardly enough for carfare and lunch money. Another offer was from a large printer, to be plant supervisor. I had no interest in that at all. The third offer was also for a rather mundane position but paid considerably more. So I went to work for the Acme Steel Company as Sales Correspondent for their Atlanta office.

My salary was not that great, but all of us at the commune were now working, so our economic stability and our lifestyle* gradually improved. We became somewhat self-conscious going places in our army-surplus jeep with the homemade body. On my way to and from work I passed the Hudson car dealer on Main Street, and each time I stared with envy at a shiny 1948 model displayed

---

*A word we would never have used at that time.

in the showroom. Automobile production had stopped during the war, and there were still waiting-lists for new cars, so T and I wondered why that Hudson remained unsold. One day we stopped to look at it close up. We had discussed the possibility of buying a Ford or a Chevrolet, but we knew this luxurious vehicle was far beyond our reach. But neither of us had ever talked with a car salesman before.

The style of the 1948 Hudson was far ahead of its time: low, sleek, rich green in color, big and imposing. We bought it jointly, owned it for years, and never had a dispute as to "who got the car." All the girls learned to drive it, and it was truly a family car. Symbolically, it transported us from poverty to plenty.

Bee had moved to East Point after leaving Wesleyan, and Daddy, Mother and Pat moved there after Daddy retired in 1950. The number of residents on Maple Street ebbed and flowed as siblings married then, in some cases, returned with their spouses. Future taxpayers were added as fast as the gestation period allowed. The number present at Thanksgiving and Christmas dinners multiplied.

No one in our expanded family became rich or renowned but neither has one been executed, imprisoned or even arrested—so far. All have provided for themselves and their families honestly and adequately.

While we lived together for so many years we naturally had a few disagreements and some very vocal disputes, but never to the point of violence, and with no profanity stronger than "dang" or an occasional shocking "damn" or "hell."

Individually, there were many disappointments, unfulfilled yearnings and heartaches, but generally we were a wholesome, happy family, laughing, playing and working together for our mutual good. Even so, none of us ever said to each other, "I love you."

Not in words.

The Stanfield home on Big Richland Creek. The name "Stanfield" in old English means "stony field," which was the name of an estate in England that William the Conqueror granted to my forebears. Big Richland Creek is a clear, rocky-bottomed stream in Humphreys County, Tennessee, where my grandfather Newton Calvin Stanfield settled about 1880. he first lived in a log cabin, then built and moved into the house pictured above in 1887. My father, five of my siblings and I were born in this house. The photograph was made about 1946.

"That tall one."
Luttie Victoria Fry, about 1910.

Charles Samuel Stanfield, about 1910. His maternal grandmother was Susannah Norman, a Cherokee Indian. In later years I thought he looked like the face on an Indian-head nickel.

Freeman, Rebecca and W. T. Stanfield, 1920 or 1921. Rebecca had just recovered from a near-fatal case of diphtheria. Shortly afterward, doctors taped radium onto her back to remove a purple birthmark. The hazards of radiation were not fully known at that time, but she evidently suffered no adverse aftereffects.

John, Bettie, and Bertha (Bee) Stanfield, about 1930. Shortly after our first move to Birmingham, we were prosperous enough for a studio portrait—the last such photograph we could afford for the next ten years.

Floyd Lee Outlaw, about 1932. An avid amateur photographer, he took most of the photos that follow. He was a good, generous man, who became the main breadwinner for his family at age fourteen. Although never unduly wealthy, he also helped my family, especially me, and in later years contributed generously to numerous charities, particularly Boys and Girls Clubs.

Freeman Stanfield with canine babysitters on the west side of the Old Home Place in 1915. My grandfather, a skilled stonemason, built the mortar-less chimney in 1887.

John, Margaret, Rebecca, Bee, Pat, and Bettie Stanfield at the Old Home Place about 1934. Photo by Floyd Outlaw.

"Me and T" about 1935.
Photo by Floyd Outlaw.

John Stanfield and J.R. Taylor on vacation in McKinnon about 1936. Photo by Floyd Outlaw.

Above: Daddy, Mother, Freeman, W.T., John, Margaret, Bettie, Rebecca, Pat, and Bee.

**Left: Daddy and Mother, about 1936
Both photos by Floyd Outlaw.**

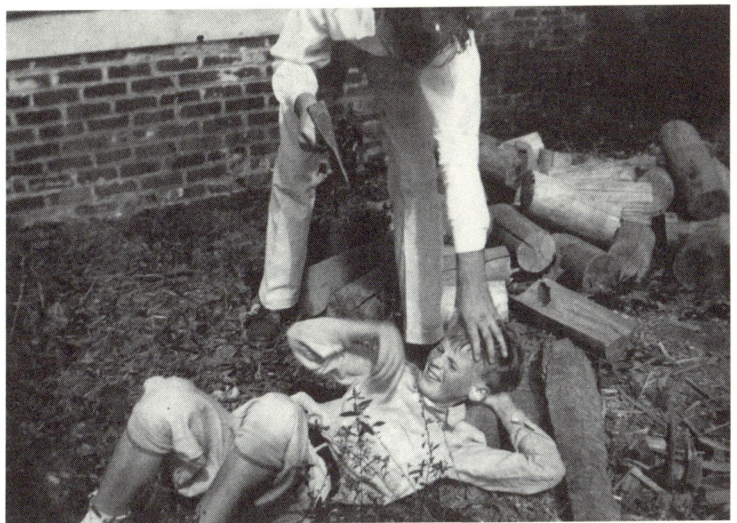
W.T. threatens to chop off my head. Probably with ample justification. Photo by Floyd Outlaw.

Bee and John Stanfield, Leon McGouirk and Oretta Yates in 1941. Photo by Floyd Outlaw.

Cousins Neal, Ray, and Billy Forrest and my right hand, about 1933. Photo by Floyd Outlaw.

John Stanfield with Jean and Jo McNeil, about 1940. On vacation at Uncle Will Fry's place in Waverly, Tennessee. Photo by W.T. Stanfield.

Captain John Stanfield, R.O.T.C. Russell High School, 1941.

Privates Joe Stanfield, John Stanfield, and Dozier Shaw, Ft. Sill, Oklahoma, 1943.

Private John Stanfield, University of Arkansas, 1943.

Pfc. Stanfield, cleaned up and shaved for R & R, Verviers, Belgium, 1945.

Postcard mailed home from German in 1945.

Tribal gathering at Maple Street, 1965. Includes all immediate family members except Daddy, who died in 1958. From top left: John, W.T., Freeman, Bettie's husband Bob Ristow, Rebecca's husband Bryan Owen, Uncle Tom, Bee's husband Bill Higgins, Pat, Bee, Bettie, Mother with Bettie's son Robin, Margaret with Bee's d'ter Betsy, Rebecca, Freeman's wife Vestine, John's wife Myra, W.T.'s wife Elizabeth, Margaret's d'ter Madelon, Bee's d'ter Patti, Bettie's d'ter Judy, Rebecca's d'ter Susan, Margaret's d'ter Pamela. Rebecca's son Sam, Bettie's son Buddy, W.T.'s son Freeman, Bee's son Stephen, W.T.'s son William, Margaret's d'ter Rebecca, Freeman's sons Bruce and John.

Epilogue

April 25, 1953, I married Myra Jo White, a Methodist preacher's daughter who lived her early years in the mountains of North Georgia and moved to Atlanta during the Depression. Her life history was somewhat similar to mine.

I continued to work for Acme Steel (later known as Interlake Steel) for twenty years even though I graduated valedictorian from Woodrow Wilson Law School and was admitted to the Georgia Bar in 1956. I have explained many times that I did not practice law because my conscience wouldn't permit it. A more honest explanation is the fact that Myra had had heart surgery a few months after we were married. At that time this was a radical, extremely dangerous procedure, and not totally successful in her case. I needed company health insurance to assure that she continued to receive the best possible medical care.

As an avocation, and for additional income, I did comedy/magic shows part time over a period of twenty years. With Myra and sometimes my sister Pat assisting, we performed for company parties, church groups and civic clubs in several southeastern states.

In 1963 Myra and I started an equipment rental business, which had grown to eight stores in three states by the time I sold it in 1990.

Myra died in 1983. The following year I wrote a 600-page manuscript, the story of her valiant and remarkable battle against heart disease. This manuscript has been read only by me but, urged by my present wife, Tolva, I hope to publish it soon under the title, *Precious Heart.*

Tolva and I were married in 1986. In 1987, when I was 65 years old, we started another business, Supply Side, Inc., specializing in the sale of products of my inventions for rental stores, caterers and the hospitality industry. During the years since then, I have patented fifteen inventions.

Ever since we married, Tolva has suffered from insomnia, which is the proximate cause of my writing this book. Many nights when she couldn't sleep, she begged me to "tell her a story," forcing me to glean my memory for stories to tell. She then insisted that I write them down for her because she usually went to sleep before I finished telling them. This doesn't bode well for the chances of this becoming a best seller—except, perhaps, as a cure for insomnia.

CAUTION:
Do not read while driving or operating heavy machinery.